T0193688

THE
LADDER
OF JACOB

It is when we notice the voice within ourselves
that we grow awareness
and manifest purpose.

Discover your inner voice!

DR. RINA STEYNBERG

BALBOA.PRESS

A DIVISION OF HAY HOUSE

Balboa Press books may be ordered through booksellers or by contacting:

Balboa Press
A Division of Hay House
1663 Liberty Drive
Bloomington, IN 47403
www.balboapress.com
844-682-1282

Because of the dynamic nature of the Internet, any web addresses or
links contained in this book may have changed since publication and
may no longer be valid. The views expressed in this work are solely those
of the author and do not necessarily reflect the views of the publisher,
and the publisher hereby disclaims any responsibility for them.

The author of this book does not dispense medical advice or prescribe the use
of any technique as a form of treatment for physical, emotional, or medical
problems without the advice of a physician, either directly or indirectly. The
intent of the author is only to offer information of a general nature to help you
in your quest for emotional and spiritual well-being. In the event you use any
of the information in this book for yourself, which is your constitutional right,
the author and the publisher assume no responsibility for your actions.

Any people depicted in stock imagery provided by Getty Images are
models, and such images are being used for illustrative purposes only.
Certain stock imagery © Getty Images.

"Our Deepest Fear" quoted with special permission from Marianne
Williamson, from *A Return to Love: Reflections on the Principles of
"A Course in Miracles,"* HarperOne, abridged edition, 2009.

Scripture quotations taken from The Holy Bible, New International
Version® NIV® Copyright © 1973 1978 1984 2011 by Biblica, Inc.
TM. Used by permission. All rights reserved worldwide.

Scripture quotations marked (NLT) are taken from the Holy Bible, New Living
Translation, copyright ©1996, 2004, 2015 by Tyndale House Foundation.
Used by permission of Tyndale House Publishers, a Division of Tyndale
House Ministries, Carol Stream, Illinois 60188. All rights reserved.

Print information available on the last page.

ISBN: 979-8-7652-2685-8 (sc)
ISBN: 979-8-7652-2684-1 (hc)
ISBN: 979-8-7652-2683-4 (e)

Library of Congress Control Number: 2022906069

Balboa Press rev. date: 04/21/2022

Contents

Preface

I started my own consulting business in 2004. I guess you could call me an entrepreneur.

Since the very beginning, I have written down every significant event that has happened to me in my business. The way the events were captured included the event (story), the emotions associated with the event, life questions asked during the time, and observations on how these life questions unfolded, solutions were found, and growth was experienced. It was all done in a journaling style.

Being a Type Five in my Enneagram profile, I can almost always objectively observe what is going on in my own life. I am the *participant* as well as the *observer* in a life experiment.

In 2008, I started to refine my technique. I would ask serious life questions and then wait for the answer to unfold. I started recognizing that the unfolding of the answer was faster when I could identify and ask a question. Around 2016, I suddenly recognized the question as well.

At this point, you may want to ask, "What do you mean you 'recognized the question'?" What I mean is, I realized that events happening to me were not random occurrences. I started exploring the idea of finding a pattern in the formation of these experiences.

I obtained my doctoral degree in 2007. Pattern recognition, research, and an enquiring mind have always been among my unique gifts. Both my master's and doctoral studies were qualitative research projects. I therefore regard myself as being skilled enough in the domain of psychological and behavioral research to observe patterns from a data set, even if that data set is my own life.

However, seeing the patterns in life events was only half of the miracle. I realized along the way that these experiences are my life lessons. The way it unfolded was that I would experience a life challenge or trauma. I would ask existential questions, the answers would unfold, and subsequently, I would experience a tremendous sense of growth. Remember that the self-help books that are easily available today were not so readily at hand then. Today we know that life lessons are meant to expand awareness, grow consciousness, and be pipelines to purpose.

Let me share what happened around 2017. The whole process had become even faster. I would get up in the morning with the life lesson in my head (almost as if I were given the research subject), the event would follow (normally a trauma), and the theory would emerge (usually from books). A sensation that the life lesson was completed would surface, immediately followed by a sense of peace. It almost felt as if I were prepared for the lesson.

It was at this point that I realized that if I resisted, the pain would be intense, but when I surrendered, the pain of the trauma would be easier to handle. It was as if I was the *participant* as well as the *observer* in the same experiment.

From an academic research perspective, *The Ladder of Jacob* can be seen as a qualitative, ontological, participative research case study, where the following definitions apply:

- **Qualitative** research is a method that includes examining a case study in order to understand a phenomenon better.

- **Ontology**, according to John Dudovskiy, can be defined as the science of study of being, and it deals with the nature of reality. Ontology is a system of belief that reflects an interpretation by an individual about what constitutes a fact. It deals with the nature of existence.

- **Autoethnography** is the study of self, where personal experiences are used to examine a phenomenon. According to Garance Maréchal, "autoethnography is a form or method of research that involves self-observation and reflexive investigation in the context of ethnographic fieldwork and writing."

So, from a scientific perspective, you can say that I have done significant research these past few years. This book is a representation of what I have studied, and I have no doubt there are many readers who want to know what I have found.

From a purely human perspective, the story is told as a novel from the viewpoint of the *participant* in the experiment (me). All the "higher" conversations and observations are noted from the perspective of an *observer*. This observer will intervene at critical times. Could the observer be my higher self or soul, observing the "me" who is living this hard life? Could it be a guardian angel, a guide, the Divine, God? It is up to the reader to decide.

All the hardships, tears, joy, wrestling, and peace shared in this novel are real events that I have personally experienced. However, to protect the identity of the wonderful people who played a role in my life events, and who have gone through pain themselves, fictional identities were chosen for individuals and companies.

I wrote this book over a period of seventeen years. Life lessons are learned over long periods of time. Although I almost completed the book in December 2019, I just could not cross the finish line. Something or someone held me back. At the time, I also wondered, what could the last life lesson be? It must be a significant one! I had promised the publisher to submit my manuscript by May 2020. Then, in March 2020, COVID-19 hit the world. Is there anything that could have been a better last life lesson for a small-business entrepreneur? I had to include the impact of this phenomenon as well.

I am sure readers can relate to most of the events and replace characters with ones from their own stories.

In the end, names and events don't really matter. What matters is the growth, while climbing *The Ladder of Jacob*.

Acknowledgments

So many people have been part of my journey. So many people played a role in this destiny. I would like to thank them all.

I would like to thank my lifelong soulmate for his encouragement. You believed in me.

Thank you to my daughter, who was two years old when I started writing this book and is nineteen now! You are such an inspiration. You have a way with words, and you encouraged and advised me so much in the writing of this book. I look at you and ask myself, how is it possible that writing comes so easy for someone as young as you, but the words disappear for me, and I'm in my fifties now? May this book serve as an example to other fifty-year-olds that it is never too late to do something totally out of your comfort zone.

I would like to thank all my colleagues who worked with me in the consulting practice. You helped me to survive all the hardships. You stood by me and watched me find myself. Thank you for your encouragement. For those who have passed on, I know we will meet again.

The consulting business I built as a vehicle to live my life purpose was the playing field on which I learned all my life lessons. I know one cannot thank a place, but I must express my gratitude to firstly Reflection and later Mind Matters Consulting (MMC) for giving me the platform for my experiment. These were the places I loved but also resented the most.

Thank you to all the people and companies who had a role in teaching me my life lessons. You might not know who you are, but you were critical in my growth journey. To protect your identity, I will not use your real names.

I would like to thank my editor, Isabel Meyer; my graphic designer, George Hugo; and my publisher, Balboa Press. You are awesome.

Lastly, I would like to thank "God." When you read this story to the end, you will discover why "God" is in quotation marks.

Message for the Reader

This story is for readers who struggle to find their life purpose and sometimes feel life does not make any sense. For you, the novel might help in finding your own meaning and peace.

It is for readers who go through hardships and don't know why. The book might be the tool for you to recognize your own life patterns and start living differently.

It is for entrepreneurs who find it hard to make a living from their businesses, and despite their best efforts, still struggle to make ends meet. May the resilience displayed in the novel light a new fire in you and spark your innovation.

It is a story of hope for my home country, South Africa, after the COVID-19 world pandemic. As our president has said, "Dear fellow South Africans … we shall recover."

Lastly, it is for readers who just love a good story. Enjoy the journey with me.

THE LADDER
OF JACOB

Genesis 28:11,12,16,17 (NLT)

Jacob found a stone to rest his head against and lay down to sleep. As he slept, he dreamed of a stairway that reached from the earth up to heaven. And he saw the angels of God going up and down the stairway.

Then Jacob awoke from his sleep and said, "Surely the Lord is in this place, and I wasn't even aware of it!" But he was also afraid and said, "What an awesome place this is! It is none other than the house of God, the very gateway to heaven!"

CHAPTER 1

A Lonely Quest

A loud ringing phone shocks me out of intense concentration as I am working on the training strategy for my company. My office is spacious and comfortable, and the big window overlooks a hedge of pink and white rosebushes framing the footpath leading to the front door of the office building.

I recognize the number of the caller. I have been expecting this call and try to steel myself against the blow of the message. "Dad is gone" is all my sister is able to say.

The words cut through my body like a cold, sharp knife. The blade slices through me in slow motion. It starts as acute pain in my head, disorienting me. The sensation moves down to contract my throat. It grips my heart with ice and sucks the air from my lungs. Nausea rises in my stomach, and my legs start to tremble. I am paralyzed and cold, feeling cut off from the life source. Then very slowly, I feel life creeping back, warm blood flowing, and heat returning to my body. Is this what shock feels like?

I mechanically phone my husband and discuss arrangements to travel to Modimolle, my parents' hometown. Although, from now on, only one parent will still be living there.

My dad had been diagnosed with cancer two years earlier. It was time for him to *go home*. The cancer had taken its toll.

Though I knew this was going to happen, you are never prepared for the death of a loved one.

Much later in the afternoon, we hit the road in a northern direction from where we stay in Secunda, a small mining town. There is a solemn silence in the car. We are each busy with our own thoughts. The road feels longer than usual today. I don't know why I am in a hurry to get there. My dad is gone, and I can't bring him back.

As we travel toward Modimolle, I stare out the passenger window and notice the open grass fields along the road. The road is so familiar, yet in my heart lies such an unfamiliar feeling. Tears are streaming down my cheeks. *My dad, who I loved so intensely, is gone! How am I going to cope with this?*

For the next few days in Modimolle, I am on automatic pilot, dealing with family, friends, and all the decisions. Nobody has prepared me for this either, but I survive. I push through the funeral arrangements and am relieved when it all eventually comes to an end. After a few more days supporting my mother, we return home.

Days and months fly past. I cut out the pain. It is too harrowing even to allow myself to begin to feel. I turn into a robot. Day after day, I just go on. I deliberately avoid thinking or feeling too much and consciously suppress the nagging anguish of grief.

*   *   *

It is already six months since my dad passed on. I am driving home after a business meeting in the city. As I watch the world outside flying by, it triggers memories of similar scenery the day we went to Modimolle after Dad had died. The similarity triggers the grief, and I start crying. I cry for Dad, who passed away, but mostly I cry for my own pain and questions that do not want to go away.

Every day, I sit in my office and wonder what life is about. *Who am I without my dad? Can a twenty-eight-year-old girl live without a father? Why do I exist? What am I busy doing? Why and for whom am I doing this?*

I know the trauma of my dad's passing is creating a million questions about life in my mind—the so-called existential questions. While my mind is grappling with all these questions, my heart starts pumping emotions of grief and sadness that create a downward spiraling tornado inside me. It is a dark hole with painfully searing emotions that leave me with more questions than answers.

As I continue driving, the road feels endlessly long, and my tears keep falling all the way home. I did not know a human being was capable of shedding so many tears.

* * *

Several months pass again after this dreadful trip from the city. I wake up one morning with a wave of indescribable anger.

My father was a religious man who had a profoundly personal relationship with God. When the pain of his cancer was unbearable, I could hear him praying to God for relief. It was never a secret that he was a man of God. I even remember with a little smile how Dad, ill as he was, would comfort the church minister when the latter was at a loss for words of compassion.

Why did a loving God leave His child in pain and let him die? I have no explanation for this, and I do not want this God to be my God any longer.

Sunday after Sunday, I go to church with anger in my heart. I am angry with this Father who does not care.

"Leave me alone, Father! I will figure out life myself. I am on a quest here, and I will figure this out on my own," I bravely declare.

Blinded by my anger, I develop arrogance. For a while, I have an answer for everything. I am good at research, so it is easy to find conceptual theories that I can quote and deploy in conversations around religion. It is easy to protect my own inner insecurity with conceptual jargon. But deep down, a little voice is asking questions, and this voice becomes louder.

*   *   *

Despite the turmoil inside me, I appear well organized and in charge of my life. I get things done. This automatic pilot mode works well for me. I achieve great success in my professional life and continue to climb the corporate ladder. This is despite my constant questioning of the intrinsic value of our human existence—questions for which I do not have any answers.

One Tuesday evening, I meet Anna, a colleague who later becomes a dear friend. In town for meetings at our offices, she is staying in a guesthouse.

Secunda, the town I live in, was established in the 1970s to host a giant fuel refinery with four coal-supplying mines. It was founded to make South Africa less dependent on the import of crude oil. Nothing much happens here, as it is more focused on the functional than entertainment, and the few shops stock only the barest of everyday necessities.

It is, therefore, somewhat ironic that it is considered one of the wealthiest towns in the province because of its industrial activities. It is also rich in human capital, as the refinery and mines employ many graduates. This makes our town rich in money and conceptual potential.

I don't think Anna, being a city girl, really enjoys her biweekly business visits to us. Accommodation for visitors here is relatively sparse and mainly caters to contractors visiting the mines and factories. Although she usually stays in the upmarket guesthouse, it still only provides for basic needs, such as a clean bed and bathroom. There is no such luxury as a restaurant on site. This results in us ending up in her room with boxes of takeaway pizza on our laps and lukewarm coffee in plastic cups.

I have my own agenda for meeting with Anna tonight. I lean forward to grab another slice of pizza, hiding my unease behind a pretense of nonchalance, and blurt out my big question: "So, tell me, Anna: who do you think is God?"

The pizza is frozen halfway to my mouth. Is lightning going to strike me dead for having uttered such a blasphemous question?

But nothing happens. There is no lightning, no voices from the sky, and I am still alive!

Anna looks at me calmly, her eyes brimming with empathy. There is no shock or disapproval. On a couple of earlier occasions, she has been part of my "help me with life" conversations and volunteered to be my life coach. She is aware that my dad has passed on and that I am suffering from all these existential questions.

However, in the ensuing silence, I suddenly wonder if my question was too blunt, too direct. The air hangs between us for a few stretched-out moments. Then Anna sighs lightly and sits back against the cushions on the ugly yellow couch. It is as if she is preparing herself for a lengthy speech.

Contrary to what I am expecting, her answer is short and sweet: "Rina, sometimes you have to leave God to find God."

I am a little unprepared for this one. *Am I leaving God? Is this even allowed? Will I burn in hell? What does she mean?*

"You see, Rina," she continues, "sometimes we define God in a particular way, and then we realize that our definition of God falls short. Then we leave that God with that definition to find God is richer, much more than the way we defined Him initially. I can see you are leaving God. You will search, and you will meet Him again."

5

Normally, such a simple explanation would not be enough for me. I usually will pepper people answering me in this manner with more questions to try to make sense of what they are saying. But the peace surrounding Anna while she is talking makes me realize that she knows what she is talking about. Her calm voice, mingling with authority in her body language, leaves me with a wish to preserve this magical moment. For the first time, I sense there is more to understand than what words can explain. My conceptual and intellectual talk will not be the right thing now.

I wait a few seconds, wondering if the wisdom will be instilled in me like a software update on a computer. But nothing happens.

After a few more minutes, I realize nothing miraculous is going to happen tonight. I guess I will have to be satisfied with the insight that I am not angry at God; I am angry because my definition of God is not working. This is it. This is what I had to hear tonight.

Anna's calm voice speaks again. "Rina, God will not change. You must change your definition of God. Go and find a new definition."

I have a busy mind, and while a million thoughts are running through my head, she patiently watches me. People can see how I think by watching the deep frown right between my eyes and lines running across my forehead. I always wear my hair with bangs because of these pronounced wrinkles, as if I was born to think deeply. When I go through a thinking process, the wrinkles become even more noticeable, and then when I have my answer, the frown disappears, and the wrinkles soften.

This, of course, is all happening while Anna is watching me right now. She is patiently waiting for my forehead to clear, which is probably not going to happen tonight.

After a few silent minutes, she yawns, and I realize it is time to go. Anna is tired, and I have a lot to think about. I decide to call it a night. "Thank you, Anna. I really needed this evening," I say while reluctantly getting up from my chair.

"You are welcome. We will talk again, but always remember not to waste your time on *why* you are leaving the old. Don't feel guilty about leaving something, rather spend your time searching for the new. Spend your time wisely. You will find the new. The quality of the search determines the quality of the answer."

I clearly hear the reassurance in her voice. Something in Anna's calm presence tells me she has found "the new." I am beginning to get the idea that it is not something you can tell somebody. It is to be one's own experience, and Anna knows it. But she is aware that I have started on the journey to discovery.

As I am leaving, Anna gives me an encouraging hug at the door, and I see the glistening of tears in her eyes. I get the idea that she knows something I am not yet privy to. I also get the idea that the tears represent some of the pain that still lies ahead for me, which stirs uneasy feelings in my bones.

As I drive home, the night feels awfully dark and lonely. Have you ever felt as if you are alone in your search for answers while the rest of the world seems to be perfectly happy where they are? Everybody looks so content and settled. They behave as if they are perfectly in control of their worlds, or maybe they just don't care. Perhaps they are ignorant. The dilemma for me is that I don't even know what I am searching for. I don't even know what I don't know.

I just realized tonight that there must be something more— that elusive "something" that I am missing. The feeling of restlessness moves in me again, while the Bible verse Psalm 42:5, *"Why are you downcast, O my soul? Why so disturbed within me?"* plays in my head over and over. It is as if I have pressed the audio looping button as I always do when I design training materials and want the music to repeat on all the presenting slides.

I arrive home safely and wearily make my way to our dark bedroom, where my husband is already peacefully asleep. Once I am in bed, the words of that Bible verse continue to loop in my head. In desperation, I pull the covers tighter around me and mentally, again and again, try to press the "stop" button to make it go away.

CHAPTER 2

The Uprooted Tree

The joyful singing of birds wakes me early as always. The first thing I do every morning is look for the sun. Is it shining? What type of day will it be?

One glance at Hubby lying snuggly in bed tells me he will not move soon. He is the practical type who checks the weather report for the next day on his mobile when he goes to bed at night. Not like me, who measures the weather for the day by the morning sun. He is also not an early riser, except when going for a scheduled run. Then he easily scoots out of bed at the break of dawn—something of which I am so envious.

I have a unique relationship with daybreak. There is magic in the silence of an early morning. I sometimes wonder if there are not angels at work at night, and just before we wake up, they wrap up their work and leave.

When I was a child, there was a delightful advertisement for cookies on television. Little elves would bake cookies in a bakery's kitchen during the night, and the following morning the shelves in the bakery would be stocked to the brim, as if by magic. Sometimes there are similar pictures in my mind of angels working on earth at night. I treasure the idea that they leave just before I wake up in the morning.

I slowly roll out of bed and stumble to the kitchen to fetch two mugs of steaming coffee. We have a special morning routine of sharing our thoughts and our coffee before starting a new day.

While I am busy getting ready to leave for the office, my mind keeps on reflecting. It is like listening to a playlist, but somehow the same song repeats again and again. When listening to music, one part of your mind can continue with routine tasks while another part will concentrate on the melody. While still busy with mundane morning routines before leaving for the office, my mind jumps between phrases and concepts related to work. Suddenly, a story slowly unfolds in my head, and I only catch bits and pieces of it here and there.

It is almost as if there are two parts to me. No, wait, there are three. The first part is busy with a journey of searching for something. Heaven knows what! Maybe it is searching for the treasure of life. It might be on its own journey, like the boy in the book *The Alchemist*.

The second me is dealing with the mundane details of everyday life: packing my bag for the day at work, getting my car keys, kissing Hubby goodbye, and safely driving to work.

But there is a third me, an observer. It is as if this entity is separate from the other two. She watches how the other two compete for attention. This third me is never intervening, always just watching.

I am crazy! How on earth can one person have three "me"s?

Maybe this is what Sigmund Freud called the id, ego, and superego, I want to ask with my background as a psychologist. Maybe in today's psychological terms, I can refer to my three "me"s as different levels of consciousness. The *higher conscious*, in my case, is my experience as an observer. Then there is my *subconscious*. I guess this part stores all my memories but also asks all the life questions that are driving me crazy and sends me on my journey of "You are on a quest, girl." Lastly, there is the *conscious* me, the one that keeps me doing what I need to do on a daily basis.

The conscious me has just alerted me that I have arrived at my office. Goodness, I can overthink stuff! It is as if my brain has its own bookshelf, stocked with many different publications. From time to time, I draw a book from the shelf, and I wrestle that subject.

I open my computer and stare at the screen. The thinking starts again. This time, I draw the book titled *Purpose*.

Purpose always starts haunting you on a specific day, and then it never stops till you find it. To find your purpose in life is a lonely struggle that tears you apart. Some people end up with depression; others die unfulfilled; and many never find their purpose. Some people search in alcohol, some in drugs, some in sex, some in money, and some in power. The point is, this is not where purpose is hiding.

"Purpose is ingrained in your own DNA," I hear myself concluding out loud. The subconscious has taken over again, and conscious is nowhere to be found. Conscious is staring blankly at the computer screen.

The subconscious continues ...

My dad's passing and my search for God sparked two critical questions in me: *Who am I* and *Why do I exist?* These are purpose questions, and I am officially searching for a purpose. We don't know in life that we are actually on a life journey where purpose is part of an unfolding story.

My real story starts much earlier in my life.

I am falling deeper and deeper into the memories that form part of my subconscious. The rational, factual, and conscious part of my brain is called the *prefrontal cortex*, I recall from my old psychology books. This is the part that keeps me in the present moment and is offline now.

The hippocampus is the part where I store and retrieve memories about everything I have ever read and experienced in my life. It allows me to learn from past experiences and anticipate what is likely to happen in the future. I am now visiting this library part of my brain.

I totally lose track of the here and the now and fall back right into an old movie scene.

*   *   *

I am fourteen years old. I am on the farm where I grew up. We are not rich, and I know we sometimes need to get on with the bare minimum, but deep down, I am happy. I am walking from the farmhouse to the *kraal* (an enclosure for cattle or other livestock). When I reach the fence, my eyes immediately search for my cow and her calf. Dad gave me this cow when she was a calf, and now she is a fully grown cow with a calf of her own. I am so proud of her.

Oh, there they are. I watch them for a while and then walk back to where Dad is milking the cows. He always wears this big, wide-brimmed hat. The South African sun is scorching, and Dad does all the farm work himself. Dad looks at me and smiles, glad to see me.

I have known for some time now that it is not going well with our family's finances. My first clue came when Dad told me that he could not afford my school fees anymore. A couple of times, I had to get up in class as part of the bunch of pupils who had not paid school fees. This is such a humiliating practice. What do teachers think they will accomplish by humiliating a child in class if the parents cannot afford to pay school fees?

Dad gets up with two pails full of fresh milk, and we slowly walk back to the old farmhouse where we live. I wish I knew the whole history of this beautiful old house. With its thick walls running through the middle, one would think it might have been an old barn or a shed in its earlier life.

We walk into the cool and shady kitchen, where Dad puts the pails of milk on the huge old oak table in the middle of the room. Mom is busy with her regular kitchen duties. We work very hard on the farm. There is no money for helpers. Dad will occasionally hire some extra hands to help with heavy farming activities, but mostly we do the work ourselves. Even the children are keen to help with farm duties, as it can be fun as well.

Some days it can be scary when you need to help tend the herd and some of the cows are being difficult and obstinate. There are also days when we must work in the fields under the hot African sun. You get tired and sunburnt, and then you just want to go home. However, it is also wonderful to enjoy farm life and see new lambs frolicking or to bring fresh eggs from the chicken coop.

Back in the kitchen, Dad looks at Mom before slumping into a chair at the well-worn wooden table.

"Rina, we cannot go on," he says.

I am lost in a world of my own, and for a moment, I am too disoriented to grasp what he is saying. What does he mean?

Dad sees my confusion and continues, "We are going to lose the farm. We don't have money to continue anymore. We tried to apply for more bank loans and every other avenue we could pursue, but we will, unfortunately, have to let the farm go."

He turns around and slowly walks away, his shoulders bent under the burden of losing our livelihood.

The words cut through my body like a cold, sharp knife. The blade slices through me in slow motion. It starts as acute pain in my head, disorienting me. The sensation moves down to contract my throat. It grips my heart with ice and sucks the air from my lungs. Nausea rises in my stomach, and my legs start to tremble.

I am paralyzed and cold, feeling cut off from the life source. Then very slowly, I feel life creeping back, warm blood flowing, and heat returning to my body. Is this what shock feels like?

I go through the next few days like an automatic robot.

I do not really care anymore when the teacher calls me to stand in class because I did not pay my school fees. How many culprits are we this week? Last week we were about eight, and today we are only three. Maybe the humiliating practice has the outcome the teacher was hoping for. I am standing right in front of the class. I am actually one of the top academic performers in class. And now I am a top performer in not paying school fees as well. Who cares?

The bell rings, and it is break time.

I wearily make my way to the pavilion on the sports fields. I sit alone for the whole of recess. News travels fast. By this time, all my friends and the whole town know that we will lose our farm. It is so embarrassing to fall from grace. I was head girl in primary school, captain of the netball team, collected many accolades and certificates for my academic achievements. And now, I am a loser. Nobody wants to be friends with a loser. I open my lunch box to eat my sandwiches, but the bread sticks dryly in my throat.

I look up at a group of boys playing some ball game on the rugby field.

They kick the ball. My heart aches.

They kick the ball. My heart aches.

They kick the ball.

Every time they kick the ball, it feels like they are kicking my heart. I am in my own miserable hell. How did I lose my friends so quickly? Is it even possible to lose all your friends? I have lost all the things that give me a sense of security. Everything that brings me joy is gone: the farm, my friends. I even lost my cow and calf. Dad had to sell them. It was false security. Who am I?

My family cannot help any more. The community rejects us. Money is gone, status is gone, friends are gone. *God, who am I, and who are You?* Everything inside me is searing pain, and tears start to roll slowly over my cheeks. I cry for myself, isolated and rejected by my friends. Alone. Nobody.

*   *   *

The movie playing in my head freezes with the picture of the young girl crying where she sits alone on the sports pavilion. I wipe the tears from my cheeks. This scene keeps on coming back, and every time it plays, I feel the deep aching pain of loneliness in my heart.

I want to erase this sad episode from my mind, so I quickly move my thoughts to more factual matters. They shift to how the brain and memory work. The hippocampus stores and retrieves short-term memories as a whole story, which includes the factual storyline or what happened, as well as the intense emotion. My question on purpose probably triggered my longer-term childhood memory. Whenever we recall these stories, we recall the emotions and bodily sensations with them. Sometimes these stories and emotions become almost unbearable, or that is at least how I am experiencing it.

It feels as if this particular memory is stored in every cell in my body. As if every cell remembers how it feels to be cut off from a community. It is almost like an uprooted tree, its roots torn and separated from the life-giving soil. The tree dies a slow death.

I remember how easy I found it back then to leave the farm at age fourteen and to go live with my sister and her family. There was nothing left for me in a town where I felt uprooted from the community. I was cast out, rejected, alone, and separated. I

15

was left to die. I was shocked and hurt deeply by how casually a community could unite and turn against somebody they regarded as an outcast. I felt like the "cursed fig tree" from the Bible.

"Why do people reject a person whom they perceive to be different from them and even tear a mere child away from her own community?" I ask out loud, shaking my head in disbelief.

CHAPTER 3

A Precious Gift

Excited, I hold out my hand for my own copy of the new matric-prescribed book. The cool smooth cover fits snugly into my hand. I cautiously bring it closer to my nose so that I can smell the book, not so obviously as to attract the attention of my matric classmates. I slowly put the book on my school desk and drink in every detail of the cover. I read the title: *Circles in a Forest*. The author is Dalene Matthee.

I force myself not to hug the book to my chest. That will definitely draw the unwanted attention of my classmates, and *that* I want to prevent at all costs.

I am in a new town, attending a new school, and I have new friends. After my unpleasant experience at my previous school, I am oversensitive about what other people think of me. During the past four years that I have lived with my sister, I have coped by always providing just enough information about myself so as not to raise eyebrows. I do not freely share my feelings, thoughts, or history. I specifically do not share my history!

I play a very clever trick on people. The moment I get the feeling that people will ask me about myself, I ask them questions about themselves. They get so excited that somebody wants to listen to their stories that they don't bother with mine any further. This wonderful survival trick carries me safely through my high school career. I protect my inner self. No sharing, no rejection. That works for me.

"Rina!"

"Sorry, ma'am."

"Are you listening? Did you hear I said you must read the first two chapters as homework?" The teacher looks a bit irritated, and I know I need to pacify her a bit.

"I will most definitely do so, ma'am!" I reply while leaning forward in my seat to show my interest and calm her irritation.

I am not a troublemaker in school. In actual fact, I think teachers would describe me as ordinary, shy, and conscientious. They might even whisper amongst themselves, "You know, the girl who has been living with her sister the past four years. Wonder what the real story is?" I can imagine how they whisper the words behind their hands as if they want to hide evil gossiping with the gesture. But luckily, nobody bothers to ask me too many questions, and I don't really care what they do behind their hands.

* * *

From the moment I open the book after school, I am captured by the story of the main character, Saul Barnard. From the very beginning, it is as if I am in the story. I can identify with every disappointment, shock, and struggle Saul is going through.

I am as disillusioned as Saul. I am eighteen years old, with a strict Calvinistic upbringing. I thought all people helped their brothers and sisters in need. Though, here I am, already exposed and betrayed by people I have trusted. They did not live up to this help-your-brother principle.

After my "uprooted tree" experience, I have started to question the world. I am seriously questioning the world! I am even more seriously questioning the *people* of this world. Maybe that is why Saul starts to feel like an old friend.

Saul Barnard also started questioning all the "beliefs" of his tribe. They believed it was not possible to escape from the forest where they lived. But Saul successfully challenged that belief. Maybe my former town and school were my forest as well. One can leave the forest, but there is always a price to pay. The price is to walk away, to walk alone, and to walk cautiously.

Hypnotized by the forest story, I continue reading how Saul started challenging the belief of the forest people that the gall of the blue duiker, a small antelope found in parts of Africa, was in its head. Saul questioned this belief and physically looked for the gall in the head of the blue duiker. He found it not to be true and then started questioning more of the beliefs and customs of the forest people.

After reading this, I shake my head. Some people will go to extremes to find the truth. However, Saul's search was fruitful. He discovered that this old belief was not true. After this experiment, Saul started questioning all the customs and his current circumstances. When he wanted to leave the forest, the community discouraged him, almost violently trying to keep him from leaving. But he knew there was a truth out there that he needed to explore, and he did.

I lower the book for a moment as I reflect. Why is it that when people see somebody who might be successful, they try to hold that person back? Even if there is the slightest chance of pursuing a dream of a better life, people will discourage it. Maybe it has something to do with, *If I cannot have it, neither can you. I feel better if you fail. Because if you manage to do it and find a way out, then I will have to also. And I am so comfortable in my current space.*

These are my theories, but why do people really do that? It is a rhetorical question that hangs heavy and unanswered in the air. I wait a few more minutes, as if I believe somebody will answer my question. Then I continue reading how Saul Barnard challenged all these conditioned beliefs from his tribe and then became a rich man after leaving the forest.

He first challenged a basic belief, and then he started challenging more serious cultural beliefs. Saul got "unstuck" by breaking from the conditioned beliefs of his tribe. Saul Barnard becomes my role model, my hero. His journey becomes my lifeline—a lifeline thrown to me by my schoolteacher, in the form of a book.

"Well, luckily, it was not thrown. The lifeline was politely handed to me by the teacher in the form of a book," I mumble to myself while getting up to fetch my lunch from the kitchen, where my sister always leaves it for me.

I settle in a chair at the dining room table. The plate of food is in front of me, and the book is propped up behind it. I continue reading between mouthfuls of macaroni and cheese.

"I have to identify what beliefs are keeping me stuck. That is what Saul did," I say to myself while walking to the kitchen with the empty plate. I grab the book on my way back to my bedroom. I am so glad that I have an excuse to continue reading. It is part of my homework. However, I have long since passed the teacher's instruction to read the first two chapters. I can't put the book down!

This is exactly how I feel at this stage of my life: stuck. I feel like an undiscovered diamond, a precious stone lying in the mud. There is so much mud around me, nobody can see who I really am. I have hidden myself, as well as the truth about where I come from, what I believe, and what I have to offer.

It is as if I am asleep. I have forgotten who I really was, even before the "uprooted tree" incident—the event when a community cut through the ties that had bound me to them and left me to shrivel up like a tree without its roots anchored in the soil. The "uprooted tree" became my description of that time when I was fourteen years old. It seems I was too complacent. I was sound asleep even before that happened.

I believed what I thought others were saying about me, and I started living that belief. I am a lamb in a flock of sheep. I follow social rules: *Don't make trouble, don't question, obey the rules. If you don't, society will dig you out again to leave you with your roots in the air.*

I start to live in fear that this might happen to me again. I am so fast asleep, I can hear myself snore! A word that better describes my state of mind rears its ugly head: *ignorant.*

*   *   *

The more chapters of the book I finish reading during the next few days, the more charged up I get. The first recognizable life lesson that crosses my mind while reading Saul's book is that the blue duiker's gall does not sit in its head for me either.

My *aha* moment is that all the rules my tribe enforced were also not necessarily *the ultimate truth*. "Well, their truth in how they treat troubled members of their tribe is most definitely warped," I mutter to myself, sitting alone in my room after school again one afternoon.

Like all the previous afternoons, the empty lunch plate is back in the kitchen, and my school dress hangs neatly in the wardrobe. My room is painstakingly neat for a teenager. I am lying on my bed while reading the book, but I will smooth out any creases the moment I get up. My other homework is already done, and my school bag is packed and organized for the next day. I have time on my hands. I am free to spend more hours reading and absorbing this book that has become so much more than homework. It has become my life work.

Every afternoon, I repeat this ritual. As the days go by and I am nearing the end of the book, something shifts in me. Years of grief, sorrow, sadness, and guilt that formed onion layers of pain come loose. Something starts to boil inside me and creates an indescribable brew of bile and anger.

"How dare they?" My cry is aimed at nobody in particular but rather a vow to myself to show my adversaries that I will uncover more truths, and I choose to survive.

From that day on, I find that there are more truths that, in actual fact, are not so true. There are also hidden truths that nobody shares. Are they intentionally hidden? Are these rules made by people who are afraid themselves? Are we molded to believe certain things to make it easier to control us? We are conditioned to comply.

"How dare they?" I ask again with the anger in me smoldering like a volcano waiting for the eruption. How is it possible that I, normally a steady and peaceful rock, can suddenly become an unstoppable angry force?

When we are angry and in pain, we look for something or somebody to blame. When the energy we suppress eventually comes loose, we want to use it with force. We want to destroy! For years, I was locked inside, suppressed, and behaved. Now, I am breaking free.

*   *   *

I take life on with a vigorous zest, afraid of nothing. That is how I approach my post-school studies. I complete my bachelor's degree, an honors degree, and then my master's degree, cum laude. I register as a psychologist. Nothing comes easy, as my parents do not have money to pay for all of this. I work full-time while continuing with my studies and get by with the barest necessities. But I am out to show the world I will survive.

I eventually start climbing the corporate ladder. I learn the law of attraction, and I start living the law of attraction. The law is based on the belief that positive thoughts attract positive outcomes and negative thoughts, negative outcomes. I decide to go for the positive. Take what you can. It is yours to take! Saul's book woke the snake in me, and it is uncontrollably dancing to the tune of success.

However, none of this brings true happiness. The tune does not resonate well with me. The questions start again: *Is this really who I am? Am I an angry and ferocious force to be reckoned with? Am I a dangerous snake dancing to the tune of success, just waiting for the perfect moment to strike and kill?*

And here ends the second reel of the movie from my early life, playing on an invisible screen in my head. It concludes with the *Who am I really?* question.

"If I am not the passive victim of circumstance, and I am not the vicious villain, then who am I?" I throw the question at the mute furniture in my office.

CHAPTER 4

A True Identity

The knock on my office door brings my attention back to the present. I am staring at my computer screen, currently in rest mode. In my mind, I was watching black and white movies from my past.

I greet Lionel as he enters. "How are you?" One of the best trainers in our training department, he does his work with infectious passion.

"May I bother you for a moment?" he asks while closing my office door.

I intuitively know he wants to discuss something serious. He would never walk into my office and close the door. He would typically stand at the door with one arm resting on the filing cabinet. That is his usual position. Something strange is going on today. I look at him with anxious anticipation.

However, he smiles to comfort me. I suddenly fear that he might want to leave my department. He is my head of training, the best in the business, and I am lucky to have him. He is the most passionate and dedicated trainer I know. I had to work hard to win him over to my department—as a matter of fact, I pinched him from the production department.

Hiring people with technical expertise is fairly easy, as is finding general trainers, but hiring passionate technical trainers is an entirely different ball game. I have spent so much time and energy coaching this man. I cannot afford to lose him.

Lionel stands like a schoolboy called to the headmaster's office who must confess to stealing a page from a teacher's notepad. He senses my growing anticipation. He then gathers all his courage and walks toward the whitecboard on the wall opposite my desk. He grabs one of the whiteboard pens, wheels around, and looks me straight in the eye, ready and determined to deliver whatever performance he has planned.

"I want to share something with you," he starts his speech.

I begin to relax. I get the idea that this will be serious, but at least not something to worry about.

"I want to explain to you how a diamond-cutting process works," he says.

For a split second, I think he has lost the plot. But then, everything up to now was very strange. So, I decide to hear him out. I have some spare time, and it might be interesting to hear what he has to say. I give him a *yes* nod. I think he saw my moment of hesitation.

He immediately assures me by saying, "You will only understand at the end. Please allow me my full explanation."

I give him another *yes* nod.

The next moment, Lionel starts talking with a flare of passion like I have never seen before. It is almost as if a fire is burning inside of him.

"Years before this company employed me, I worked at a diamond mine. Have you ever had the opportunity to see a raw diamond?" he asks.

I wish I could say yes, and I would not mind seeing one. However, I have to shake my head.

"Well," he continues, "a raw diamond is quite an unimpressive stone, looking like a common rock. It has dirt around it, and one cannot see it is a diamond. Only specially trained people know it is a diamond. The man on the street will not recognize it as a diamond and will step on it without paying attention. Nevertheless, these ordinary-looking muddy rocks are taken to the diamond factory, where a specialist will study the stone and decide what will be the perfect cut." He halts, letting this last piece of information sink in first.

Then he continues, "You see, a diamond has specific potential, and this potential needs to be exposed as much and as best as possible."

He shifts his weight from the right foot to the left foot. "If you cut away too much, you lose some of the value of the diamond. The diamond is measured, and then it is cut according to a precise cutting plan. First, the big cuts are made. This operation is very delicate because if the diamond is cut incorrectly, it is worthless. After this, a few minor cuts are made before the polishing process starts. All these processes rely on specialists in their fields, including the planners, the cutters, and the polishers. Only after all these highly specialized processes are completed is the diamond ready and its full value and beauty revealed."

Lionel makes a few drawings on the whiteboard as he explains the process. Pure energy flows from him while he is talking. I was not aware that he had worked in the diamond business before or that he knew anything about diamonds at all. To be quite honest, I see a part of Lionel that I do not know.

Lionel is on a roll. This is the thing with trainers. They have a passion for their work, and their energy is contagious. Suddenly, a bolt of energy hits me too.

"You see, Rina," he continues, "that is the magic of diamonds: no two diamonds are the same."

I make a note in my head of this new information. To be honest, I don't even like diamonds. I never read about diamonds. I do not wear diamonds. I prefer gemstones like emeralds and sapphires—green and blue stones are my favorites. My wedding ring is an emerald set in gold, and on my right hand, I always wear a sapphire ring. I look at my rings. I never realized diamonds were so fascinating.

"Rina, do you know that diamonds have different colors?" asks Lionel. He pauses to wait for my response.

"No," I reply quickly. I feel like a schoolgirl who is caught out for daydreaming. I draw my attention back to Lionel and his explanation, which is now an advanced training lesson in the diamond-cutting process.

"Well," he resumes, "there are four Cs that determine the value of a diamond. *Cut* is the first one. Apart from a cut diamond's shape, like round, heart, marquis, and so on, it is the proportions of a diamond we are interested in. When a stone is cut too shallow or too deep, the light that enters through the top is allowed to escape through the diamond's bottom and does not allow the full beauty of the diamond to be realized."

He moves his weight to the other foot again as he carries on. "Secondly, there is *color.* Diamonds come naturally in every color of the rainbow, but a colorless diamond allows light to pass through it easily, resulting in beautifully dispersed light.

"Thirdly, there is *clarity.* The clarity of a diamond is determined by the amount and location of flaws or blemishes. Most diamonds contain minute birthmarks known as *inclusions.* An inclusion can interfere with the light passing through the diamond. The fewer the inclusions, the more beautiful and valuable the diamond will be.

"Lastly, there is the *carat*. This is the weight of a diamond, measured in carats. As the carat weight of a diamond increases, so does its rarity and, therefore, its price. Two diamonds can be of equal carat-weight, but their value can differ significantly due to their cut, color, and clarity."

Lionel halts his lecture and replaces the whiteboard marker in the container. He is hereby signaling the end of his detailed explanation of diamonds. He picks up the board cleaner to wipe his notes off the whiteboard but changes his mind. I carefully watch him while silence hangs in the room. He is obviously giving me time to absorb all the technical details, as I am trying to process all the diamond information as fast as possible in my head.

"Lionel, this is fascinating," I say. "I never realized that diamonds are so pure, so complex, so special, so unique, and that the process to find the true value of a diamond is so intense and specialized. This is a lot to wrap my head around."

"I am quite aware that you don't know this about diamonds," he says, "but you definitely know this about people!"

Pow! His comment hits me right between the eyes. What on earth is he shooting at?

"Rina, that is the reason why I wanted to talk to you today. I want to say thank you because that is what you did for me. When everybody thought I was just an ordinary rock covered in mud, you saw the true diamond in me," he says. His eyes burn with intensity as he looks straight at me.

He continues, "You discovered me where I was working in the production department. You cut me like a precious diamond. You always knew what to cut away to expose my optimal value. I did not even believe in myself, but you saw my potential. People misused and underestimated me, but you noticed me. You found something in me that everybody else was missing. Now I am forty years old and settled as a trainer—a job I love and which you have groomed me for."

At the mention of his age, I instinctively want to look at his mop of grey hair, but his eyes keep mine locked in.

He steps closer to my desk and stabs a finger at his own chest. "You saw that there was a trainer in me. You made me the trainer I am today. Training is my love and my life. I am happy and energized, and every day I know I add value to our department and the factory as a whole."

Lionel points out the window, with the board cleaner he is still clasping in his one hand, in the direction of the factory buildings outside. "I cannot thank you enough, Rina. That is why I wanted to explain the diamond process to you, so you can understand what you have done for me. Thank you!" he declares passionately.

For a few moments, I am so stunned, I am unable to reply. I watch as he turns toward the whiteboard to replace the board cleaner. He is quietly observing my reactions over his shoulder. My heart is racing, beating like a huge drum, the noise in my ears so loud, I am almost afraid he can hear it.

The most gracious words anybody has ever said to me, and here I am, unable to handle it. What should I say? I am his manager and mentor. Lionel is obviously expecting some sort of reply. I pull myself together, look him straight in the eye, and say the words I feel in my heart. Almost a whisper, but still audible: "That was beautiful."

Lionel starts laughing, and I feel the tension of the moment leaving my body as well. I also start smiling.

"For months, I have been gathering my courage to come and thank you. I was so scared you would reject what I wanted to say to you, but I had to say it!" he blurts out.

I can feel his genuine sincerity and realize that this diamond speech has been in rehearsal for some time. "No, Lionel," I assure him. "This was truly the most beautiful story I have ever heard."

He gives a wide, happy smile. Is it my imagination, or did he just square his shoulders and push his chest out a bit more? He turns like a foot soldier and marches out of my office without any further ado. I hear his footsteps die away as he proudly marches down the hallway. I can't decide if Lionel is proud of the fact that he finds some meaning as a trainer or proud of his speech, which he obviously practiced for months. But he is definitely proud of himself. I smile as I glance back at the notes on the whiteboard. I am pleased that he didn't wipe it out.

I am glad about the silent space he left behind. I just want to sit in this space for a little longer. This moment in my life is the first step in finding my own reason for existence. It is as if an unseen hand lifts the veil for me, and I catch a fleeting glimpse of my true self.

I never get a chance, though, to phone Anna and tell her that I think I have found something of that new God she was talking about.

Time passes quickly when you head a department in a big corporate business while at the same time hatching plans to start up your own consulting company. I have decided to take the huge step to start my own business. I want to discover more diamonds and make a difference in the lives of many more people.

CHAPTER 5

An Intense Calling

Purpose is not a request. It is a life mission. When you send a soldier on a mission and he gets lost, you will search for your soldier till you find him. Then you will remind him of his mission. Purpose is ingrained in our DNA. It is not a choice. It will haunt you. Not living your purpose will cause you to be depressed, ill, directionless, and meaningless. That diamond inside you will burn like a fire. If you do not let it out, it will burn you up inside.

I finish writing this in a journal-size book I keep on my desk for my work notes. I like writing stuff down. Writing seems to sharpen my focus on issues I am exploring or developing, and the words on a page make me see things so much clearer. When I reread what I have written, I am sometimes astonished by how my words transpire on paper.

How does this actually happen? There must be a wise voice inside all of us. If we start writing everything down, I am sure we will find a treasure chest. But my notes are all over, in different notebooks and in different places. Today, they are in my work notebook. Maybe I must collect all these notes and put them in one book. It might make for interesting reading every now and then.

I close the notebook and put it next to my desk calendar. The page this month shows a wonderful photo of a huge elephant in the African bush. It is already October 2004.

It intrigues me how long we can be in denial about being. My excuse is that I was not issued a life manual. I am not always sure what the next step in my life should be. Sometimes I just stumble over it by accident. Why do other people always seem to know where they are heading? And then make it look easy to boot.

The only thing I know for sure is that something burns inside me so intensely that I cannot concentrate on my work. There are many different life fires: relationship fires, circumstance fires, economic fires, and political fires. But the most dangerous fires are those fires burning inside us. Nobody on earth can help me with my fire. I can only help myself.

A knock on my office door brings me back to the present. Andrew ambles in with his usual friendly grin. It is our routine once-a-month work discussion. Anybody working in a corporate environment knows about these monthly one-on-one meetings. This is when you find out if you are on track with key performance outputs, and of course, whether you have delivered on promises made the previous month.

I offer Andrew a cup of freshly brewed coffee, which he gladly accepts, a welcome change from the canteen coffee he normally drinks. "Andrew, I have something very important to discuss with you," I jump in unceremoniously.

"Yes, yes, Steyntjies, that is why I am here. Lots to discuss."

Steyntjies is his nickname for me. He prefers using surnames when talking to colleagues. He is such a good man. How will he react to what I am going to say?

"Andrew, I am resigning." I wanted to soften the blow, but it was too late. I have blurted it out.

His face turns white as he looks at me in complete astonishment and blindly grasps at a chair behind him. For a moment, I fear he is going to faint, but then he finds the chair and slowly sinks into it.

To make a long story short, I resign from my perfect job, with my perfect future, my perfect boss, my perfect colleagues, and my perfect team—and of course, my perfect salary. All in the name of a not-so-perfect purpose.

*   *   *

I design logos and letterheads and read anything I can lay my hands on about creating my own business. Having worked in human resources for almost ten years, I have never had the opportunity to learn about the business side of things. As a human resources practitioner, I arrogantly think I know all about business, but I don't. All I have is a dream and another man's word that I have the ability to "recognize and unlock potential" and "let the diamond shine." That becomes my slogan for a while.

I choose the name *Reflection* for my new business because it symbolizes what I would like to create: an environment where people can reflect on their past, present, and future and learn and grow from that knowledge.

The newly designed logo has a small figure literally "reaching for the stars," or diamonds, or at least something shiny. I think it is looking pretty cool!

And then ... reality sets in. A business is not about cute little logos or fancy letterheads. I start off by putting all legal matters in place and even obtain my company registration number. But in the end, I do not have the guts or gall to dive into the deep waters of becoming a real entrepreneur.

I am such a coward, a disappointment to myself.

*   *   *

So, I leave the corporate world only to agree to work for another consulting company. In 2005, I facilitate so many emotional intelligence (EQ) workshops that I could repeat the theory in my sleep. I learn a library's worth of theory and tools to help me set and reach my goals.

This helps a lot financially, because I get the new car I want; we buy a beautiful holiday home in the bush and live the good life. But I am nowhere nearer to my own life work, my own purpose. And the fire inside me is still burning.

Today, I am attending a session with the leadership team of the consulting company for which I am doing the EQ freelance work. The whole team is present, even one of the senior partners who is not around often. I have not engaged with him a lot in the past, and I do not know him very well. However, there is something about Danny that fascinates me. He does not speak often, but I find that it is worth listening when he does say something.

During a break in the lecture, when the others have gone outside for a few minutes of fresh air, Danny and I find ourselves alone in the conference room. While I am fiddling in my laptop bag, he seems similarly occupied. We both look up at almost the same time. What an awkward moment.

To break the uncomfortable silence, I blurt out, "I wish they included more information on purpose and meaning in the purpose module of the EQ course. The module on purpose in the EQ course is sort of meaningless and poor in information."

I am painfully aware of having repeated myself and that it is a strange remark filling a semi-embarrassing moment. However, it seems as if he has expected the comment, because he casually replies, "Yes, I always build my own theory into that module."

"Oh, and what is your own theory?" I ask with surprised curiosity.

"Are you interested in the theory of purpose?" is his counter-question.

"Yes, it would be helpful," I say while at the same time trying to keep a nonchalant posture. I don't want to look overeager.

"Read the book *In Pursuit of Purpose.* Myles Munroe is the author."

"Thank you, Danny," I say while wondering what I can ask next. But I find to my own surprise that I don't have anything else to add.

"It is my pleasure," he says and, at the same time, turns around to leave the venue through the door right behind him.

I guess that is it. It is the end of this very professional conversation. Maybe he realizes that he also needs some fresh air. Perhaps he knows these few words were enough. He grasped that his mission was accomplished. He had to deliver the message and leave, and that is what he is doing right now.

I watch his back as he walks out the door. Anxiously, I grab my pen and notebook to jot down the title of the book and author. This is a lifeline I cannot afford to lose or forget.

*   *   *

In my own personal quest for purpose, I have read about twenty books on the topic. Even if there was only one sentence referring to purpose, I would read the book. Now it seems I have missed this one.

I order the book online and have to wait impatiently for it to be delivered. When the parcel eventually arrives, I finish the book in only two days. The book is indeed a fresh perspective on life purpose. I believe that I am close to defining my own purpose, and the book is helping me figure out the missing pieces. The wisdom that Munroe shares become part of my fundamental belief system about purpose. I read some of the sections so many times that I could repeat them in the middle of the night if you would wake me.

Before I can help myself, I whisper words from the book: "To remove your purpose would be to significantly change who you are, because your purpose both informs and reveals your nature and your responsibilities. Everything you naturally have and inherently are is necessary for you to fulfill your purpose. Your height, race, skin color, language, physical features, and intellectual capacity are all designed for your purpose."

This is it. It sounds so simple. You have a specific mission on earth. You are designed for your mission. Every characteristic you have is in line with your life purpose. Every person on earth is unique with a unique purpose. Did Lionel not say this to me in 2003 already, when he told me the diamond story? This is so exciting, to get affirmation at long last. But how and where do I live this purpose? Is this consulting business the way forward?

I have figured out a few handy things about purpose. Firstly, something of this purpose burns like a fire inside me and never lets me rest. Secondly, from the theories, I figure it must be something very specific. Lastly, from what Munroe says, I am uniquely designed for it. But it is tough to figure out the exact *what* and *how*.

A sense of frustration is building up in me. Maybe it is not frustration. It might actually be energy building up. Perhaps it is the same kind of energy that people experience before bungee jumping from bridges or parachuting from airplanes. When you are an outstanding athlete, there is this boost of energy in the anticipation right before the start of the race. Because the outcome of the race is still unknown, this buildup of energy causes a restless impatience.

Why are you downcast, O my soul? Why so disturbed within me? The familiar restless words are looping in my head again and stir my restless energy even more.

There are two conflicting states in me. My fear of the uncertain future is causing a state of paralysis, making it difficult to act. But at the same time, the dissatisfaction with the current state is causing an urgency to act. Jumping between these two conflicting ideas of paralysis and action is adding to my built-up frustration.

In psychology, we refer to this as a state of *cognitive dissonance*. It is that tension between what you want and where you currently are. The brain cannot hold two conflicting ideas at the same time. It wants to choose.

I am aware of my current situation, and I know I should move on. I try to visualize a future state, but contrary to what theory asks of me, I struggle to visualize the future clearly. Maybe it is the veil of fear preventing me from "seeing" clearly. That leaves me in this weird state. This state I start to name, *Why are you downcast, O my soul? Why so disturbed within me?*

A limbo mind state. A stuck state.

Then the energy bursts.

Like a water pipe in which the water pressure is too high.

The energy spouts in all directions.

It is the moment when I jump, the moment when I act.

I know it is the right decision.

It is the year 2006.

I am totally on my own.

In my own consulting business.

I have to swim.

CHAPTER 6

The Destroying River

As I turn off from the main road, I try to recognize street names on my right. The directions said to turn right, apparently a small side street that is easy to miss. I have a meeting with the editor of my doctoral thesis. He had indicated that I must be careful, as the turnoff is easy to miss.

The past four years have been hectic. My daughter was born in 2002, the same year I started my doctoral degree. In 2004, I left the company where I was the organizational development manager. Now it is already 2006. This is the year I decided to make my grand move to go all out with my own business and to finalize my doctorate.

I am tired.

Everybody has warned me that completing a doctorate and having a baby and then, on top of it all, trying to kickstart a business is a bit too much. But here I am. My daughter is four years old. My doctorate is almost done. In effect, my doctorate is also four years old! Now I am on my way to the editor who needs to whip my thesis into shape. As far as my business is concerned, I am still surviving.

But I am tired.

My instinct seems to tell me that the turnoff must be close. I slow down. The car is a rental, not familiar to me at all. We still live in Secunda, approximately 170 kilometers from Pretoria. I have a long to-do list today. This being a good opportunity to bring my husband's car to the city for a service, I dropped it off this morning and picked up the small rental to use for the rest of the day.

My daughter, Katy, is in the car with me. We are planning a visit to her grandma, who happens to live in Pretoria, later today. So many things to take care of in one day!

I am so tired.

We must be very close to our destination now. For some reason or other, I have let Katy sit in the front passenger seat, something I never do. We believe children must sit in the back because it is safer. Now Katy is sitting next to me, safely buckled up as always. She is holding the map for me, this being the days before GPS and Satnav. We must be very close to the turnoff.

"Let Mommy see the map," I ask her. Katy holds the map for me to see. As I glance down at the map, I see the street where I need to turn right. My conscious thinks about turning right, but something different is happening.

There is an eerie awareness of a crashing sound, a painful head bang, turning-turning-turning before everything is silent.

The car is facing the opposite direction we came from. *Katy!* In a daze, I look to my left to see if my little four-year-old is OK. Pale as a sheet, but she is fine, thank God. I slowly climb out of the car.

The next thing I know, the Emergency 24 vehicle arrives, and two paramedics run toward us. It was heaven-sent that Katy was in the front passenger seat. I think this saved her life.

I am in zombie mode and respond automatically to the paramedics' questions and instructions. Operating on automatic pilot, I move the damaged car out of the way, provide our details, and even manage to report the accident to the nearest police station.

Somewhere along the line, I remember to phone my husband, my editor, and the car rental company. On the outside, I say the right things and manage to do all the right things, but inside I have fallen into an abyss of emotional stupor.

*   *   *

It is six months after the accident. I am still doing my best to make a success of my consulting business. Having just visited a client, I am on my way back to my own office. While scanning the parking lot for my car, I suddenly have trouble putting one foot in front of the other. My left foot feels frozen, refusing the move, but I somehow manage to make it to my car.

I have noticed these past few weeks that there is something wrong when I am walking, but I thought it was just a passing thing. With so many things on my plate, I don't have time to waste on little niggles. But today, I am struggling.

Now that I think about it, it has almost become a habit to look for the closest parking spot to the shopping mall entrance or buildings where I have business appointments. This frozen foot is not a new thing. I have ignored it for some time and gotten used to it. But now I realize this is not normal, and I will need to do something about it as soon as possible. While surviving in absentia from myself, I neglected my own body.

At the third ring, the doctor's receptionist answers. Our general practitioner is available, and I can come to the consulting rooms immediately. Now that I am aware of my leg, I notice how difficult it is to drive. I wonder what is wrong while finding parking right in front of the consulting rooms.

"I can't find any physical reason why your leg is playing up. But with the bump to your head in that car accident six months

40

ago, I am referring you to a well-known neurologist. Let's see if we can get an appointment for you as soon as possible," says Dr. Verster, our GP.

*   *   *

My husband accompanies me to the specialist. They are apparently going to perform many tests on me, and I need his emotional and physical support. The tests are tiring. Some of it even requires needles pressed into my leg muscles.

To the neurologist, the diagnosis is apparently a straightforward conclusion. To me, however, it is completely confusing.

"You have dystonia in your left leg. Do you know what it is?" the neurologist asks.

Sneeringly I want to say, "Of *course* I don't know what it is, doctor. How the hell would I know what it is?" Instead, I politely reply, "No, doctor, I don't know what it is, but is there anything we can do about it?"

He explains his diagnosis in sketchy detail and then suggests I use Google for more information. However, what I manage to deduce from his rather inadequate explanation is that dystonia can be brought on by head trauma, much as I experienced in the car accident six months earlier.

"You can come for Botox injections," he suggests. "It will relax the muscle, and it might help you to walk easier. The effect of the injection will last for about four months, and then you will have to repeat the process. The injections are costly. You have to get permission from your medical aid to pay for the injections, or you must pay cash."

It is interesting how the payment terms can always be explained in the clearest detail, I sarcastically think to myself. Fortunately, we belong to an excellent medical aid fund, so I opt for obtaining authorization for the Botox injections.

"One last question, doctor. Will it spread?" I anxiously ask.

"I don't know," he answers.

Now that was helpful, wasn't it?

*   *   *

The dystonia continued to worsen, so much so that I decide to finally call the medical aid. "Good morning. I need authorization for a medical procedure," I politely explain to the fund representative. I provide my medical aid number and the details of the required procedure.

Apparently, Botox is not associated with medical procedures but rather with cosmetic procedures, and therefore the medical aid does not pay for it.

Having done my Google homework, I try to explain that Botox has been developed to treat medical issues such as dystonia. No luck. The fund representative just continues to tell me that medical aid does not pay for cosmetic procedures. I undertake to forward her the neurologist's motivation, explaining the urgency of the procedure to enable me to walk properly again.

A day later, I phone the medical aid again. The answer is the same. The medical aid does not pay for a cosmetic procedure.

At that moment, I snap. I lose all reasoning and start screaming at her. "This is not a cosmetic procedure! I cannot walk. Botox was developed for people like me, not for people with vanity issues. I cannot help that they misuse a medicine meant for serious diseases. It is a serious disease if you cannot walk."

"Sorry, ma'am, this is our policy," is her cold, polite answer.

I throw the phone down. I start to tremble uncontrollably. Suddenly, all the tiredness and emotions I have kept bottled up for so long explode inside me. I begin to cry. Heaving with sobs, I cry for the many months of hard work, for always being deathly tired. I wail with feelings of guilt because I could have caused injuries to my child in the car accident. I weep for the loss of so much money, as we had to pay a significant penalty to the car rental company, the accident apparently not covered by the insurance.

The questions and thoughts threaten to overwhelm me. Why will the medical aid not help me? We cannot afford to pay for this expensive treatment ourselves. I cannot expect the money to come from our family budget. Is this disease going to spread to my other leg as well? I am so afraid. What will happen to my business if I am unable to walk? Why is the medical aid world so unhelpful?

My mind is all over the place, and I am nowhere near any clear answers. I continue to wallow in despair for a few more hours.

The finale to the Botox drama is that my wonderful husband finds the money to pay for my injections. I go for a couple of these and then read a fact sheet on Botox. Being better informed on the matter, I decide to stop the treatment.

*   *   *

Something slowly starts to sneak into my life. At first, it goes unnoticed. It is a thought that initially seems innocent enough. I start repeating this thought, unaware that it is growing into a thought pattern. And even more obscure, the fact that this niggling thought is attracting similar notions.

Donald Hebb said, "What fires together, wires together," also known as Hebb's rule.

My thoughts crystalize into beliefs. The beliefs congeal into a mind-state system. The mind-state system becomes my absolute truth, which subsequently negatively informs my life attitude. With every decision I take, I associate so strongly with this pessimistic and gloomy mind state that I become severely depressed.

Every word that leaves my mouth is negative. Everything I need to do is an effort, and I let everybody around me know that it is. I find fault with everything people around me do.

Every day I slide deeper and deeper into this downward spiral of a depressed mind state. I feel useless and worthless, and the more I feel this way, the more I treat others the same. I treat them as if they are useless and worthless objects. I project my pain onto the people around me, at work and at home.

But I am still deeply loved.

First and foremost, by the man I am married to. He does not know how to help me, but he supports and embraces me with his love. Secondly, I know I am deeply loved by the Universe—all and all, a winning combination. And then the Universe conspires with Hubby to help me by sending me a book. Hubby returns from a business session with *The Monk Who Sold His Ferrari* by Robin Sharma.

"They gave out these books at our session today. Read it. They say it is good," he says with eyes filled with love as he puts the book on my night table.

*   *   *

Soon after, we take a trip to our holiday retreat, close to Kruger National Park. There, in the tranquil bush and close to nature, I eventually find the time to read about the monk and his Ferrari. While reading the book, somewhere deep inside me, something moves. It is that first flicker of hope.

I realize that the darkness is not around me. The overwhelming darkness is engrained in my thoughts. I have created my own mind cage, and my negative dark thoughts are ensnared in this cage.

Renew your thinking is the message of *The Monk*.

I find a Bible text in Ephesians 4:23-25 (NLT) to support this: "Let the Spirit renew your thoughts and attitudes. Put on your new nature, created to be like God—truly righteous and holy. So, stop telling lies. Let us tell our neighbors the truth, for we are all parts of the same body."

I start the process of my own renewal by putting on my takkies. *Is it only in South Africa we call them takkies?* I wonder while tying the laces of my running shoes. All of this happens as if in slow motion, because I am not totally convinced of my choice to go running with a foot that can barely walk.

"I am coming with you," declares Hubby.

This offer is gladly accepted, because if I faint along the way, at least there is somebody who can phone for an ambulance. Apart from my wobbly foot, I am also overweight. Months of believing I'm not good enough for anything, combined with moping around and inactivity, have taken their toll on my hips. If you don't care about yourself, you don't care what you eat. A feeling of depression leads to unhealthy eating habits. If you are angry with your own body, you don't care for it.

"I am ready," I say. I am stating the obvious, but I say it nevertheless to convince myself. We walk outside.

"What do you want to do?" asks Hubby.

"One block," I make a circle with my finger. "I just want to go around the block," I say bravely.

Runners' dystonia, which is the correct name for my disorder, is a spasm that presents in the motoric movement of walking or running. So, as soon as I attempt to run, I immediately experience a dystonic muscle spasm. This results in my left foot contracting inward, almost tripping up my right foot in the process. An added painful discomfort is my toes curling inward against my shoe, hurting because of the resistance of flesh against rubber.

The monk survived a heart attack. I can survive a muscle attack. I gamely give another step and another and another and another. Good neurotransmitters, of which I believe dopamine and endorphins might be some, release in my body. They are causing my body to develop a form of resistance against the pain.

The frustration is still there, however. Running looks so easy, but for a person with runners' dystonia, it feels as if the foot has a mind of its own.

It does what it wants.

No thought can control it.

It is a fight against myself.

I try to control less and develop a thinking rhythm with the running rhythm.

I try to let it flow more.

It releases a bit.

It becomes easier.

Lesser control.

It releases more.

I go very slow.

My body likes the slowness and lesser control, the sense of flow.

We are nearly back home.

Slow, flow ...

Lesser control.

The more I control, the more the resistance.

The more the flow, the more the release.

I am over-controlling.

I should flow more with life.

Life is like a river. It has its own flow.

When I flow with the river, it is the water of life. We are one flowing river. It flows with me and through me. But when I see myself to be separate from the river, trying to control its flow and to swim against its current, its flood is destroying, drowning me. When I try to break away from the river, the river perceives it to be resistance. What you resist persists and is met with an equal counterforce.

When I allow the river its flow, its destroying force dissolves. It naturally raises me above the water and shows me the beauty and life the water sustains. The river and I are then one.

We arrive home. I made it! I am exhausted, but I am ecstatic. This new feeling of happiness inside me helps to dissolve some of the dark notions of depression.

I know the dystonia might never go away, but all the fears surrounding it disappear. Dystonia becomes my reminder to trust the flow of the river of life.

Chapter 7

A Clear Instruction

Do I overanalyze things? Am I, by nature, a person who tests everything? Maybe I should have become a scientist. I love to experiment with things.

I page through the Bible and decide to play my favorite game. The game is to ask a question and see where the Book falls open. The answer is then somewhere on that page. There is nobody at home, so I ask the question out loud: "What is my purpose in life?"

The Bible falls open at Matthew 10:8: "Heal the sick ... Freely you have received, freely give."

For a moment, I am stunned. This is not a joke. This is a clear message. I feel a buzzing sensation in my head. The silence swirls around me in the room like a sheet of white noise, and then suddenly, the words reverberate inside me. It is a calling: this is my purpose. There is no specific order to the words, but the message is clear to me: "... with the following instruction ... heal the sick ... freely you have received, freely give. The Kingdom of Heaven is near or within you."

With great care, I transcribe the text verse in my life journal. My scribbled notes were always all over the place. So, since 2004, when I left the corporate world, I have saved all these life notes in one special notebook. It feels as if I have just had a serious conversation that included explicit instructions. But what should I be doing? Because I don't know, it probably means I don't have the complete answer yet.

I am quite a movie buff and can recall a few movies where the hero, sitting in a departing airplane, only at that point receives final instructions for his upcoming mission from Control or the head office. My incident with the Bible verse has a similar mission-instruction feeling to it. I have a broad contract and have done some training already. My degree in psychology and my experience in the corporate world must count for something. However, the full details of my mission are still unclear.

Great excitement bubbles up inside me. How many times have I felt the presence of purpose but without the foggiest idea of how to fulfill it? This time there is more information, and I know my search for the *how* is going to continue in earnest.

It is almost as in the movies I mentioned—I have had contact with my head office today. I was only given a one-liner before communication was broken, and I will have to find the details of my mission myself by trial and error. There was no indication of the when, where, who, and how. In fact, I am not even sure what *heal the sick* really means.

* * *

At this point, I have been in the consulting business for three years. And even now, I cannot figure out the answer to my mission, or even to my own business, for that matter. Every book I read tells me how easily money will come your way when you live your purpose. But I barely survive financially, and I am constantly under immense stress to make ends meet. The frustration this causes is enough to make me want to give up.

I continue to struggle along in this rut for another long year. Sometimes I begin to wonder if I really had that Bible conversation about purpose and mission. My mind races with questions on the where and when and how. What should I do? The nightmare starts all over again, and I am nowhere near finding the answer. It is as if I am walking in a vast dry and sandy desert and my supplies are running low with no oasis in sight. In my business world, these supplies mean finances, energy, clients, ideas, and products.

Having a purpose statement is scary because it feels as if I should go and do something, but I do not know what to do. It feels as if I am misaligned with my mission. I have arrived at a destination, but the resources to complete the mission have run out. It actually feels as if my airplane has arrived at the wrong airport.

Heal the sick.

What does it even mean?

Mysterious.

*   *   *

I am sitting in front of my computer. As usual when there is a bit of stress in my life, my wobbly leg lets me know. The runner's dystonia is again getting worse by the day, and I not only struggle to run but it is also starting to impact my normal walking.

I am the first one at the office today. The building is cocooned in silence. The stress of making my consulting business financially viable is almost suffocating. How is it possible that I am still struggling to make ends meet after four years? Am I a fool to keep on trying? This struggle is causing me so much stress. And the pressure is showing in my leg, as I am really struggling to walk today.

As my mind wanders aimlessly, I fiddle around with the computer mouse. Yes, the dystonia is definitely at its worst today.

"How is my brain communicating to my leg?" I ask out loud.

Bang! Now that was an unintentional question to the Universe. Suddenly, a book appears on my screen: *Quantum Healing: Exploring the Frontiers of Mind/Body Medicine* by Deepak Chopra. I cannot remember surfing the internet or searching for information at all. I was merely absentmindedly twiddling the mouse.

I quickly navigate to the Amazon site, and before one can say *knife*, the book is mine. On its way. In the post.

I consider the search for my purpose—or rather, what I think I need to do as a purpose—and the search for a cure for my dystonia as two separate and unrelated matters. While I am trying to figure out how to help myself and my own health, I still have to make a living from a consulting business in financial distress.

However, I am optimistic and have developed a lot of resilience after my previous traumas. So, here I am, still going strong. Depending on the most pressing issue of the day, that is where I aim my focus. It is almost as if my life is divided into little boxes. With the Chopra book on its way to me, I can close the health box for now. I will deal with dystonia when the book arrives.

I open the purpose box again. Somehow, I manage to put the purpose box and consulting box next to one another.

There must be a link between these two, I say to myself. *What must I do? Please, I am ready. Show it to me?* I beg nobody in particular, as I write down the questions in my journal, a habit by now.

I get a sense that I should randomly open my Bible again. Habakkuk 2:2 simply spells out the answer: "write down the revelation and make it plain on tablets." Really? Write down what?

I phone Ethan, my former colleague and now a dear friend. He is a good coach and always has wisdom to share. Maybe he can help. Ethan invites me for coffee at his office, and we arrange to meet soon.

*   *   *

A few days later, I meet Ethan at his office as agreed. When I walk in, I notice the cramped space and sparse contents in his small cubicle. How does he still manage to work for a corporate entity? He does not really fit the mold of the corporate world.

After exchanging a few niceties and chit-chat about so-and-so, I spill the real reason for my visit. I could see he was expecting something more than just a friendly chat.

"I know my purpose in life has something to do with healing. I am trying to figure out the *what* I must do, as well as the *how*. I am also trying to figure out how it fits into the consulting business. I recently got this strange message from Habakkuk in the Bible. But I don't quite understand the message." I explain my dilemma to him, elaborating a bit on the verse from the text.

Ethan sits back with a smile and very calmly says, "It is simple. Do exactly what the message tells you to do."

"And what is that?" I ask with a serious Rina-frown on my forehead.

"You are not serious, Rina. Can you not see it? OK, let me spell it out for you: *Write it down!*" he says while leaning forward.

"What should I write down?" I ask, heavily confused now.

"Well, everything," he says. "Everything you know about purpose and healing, pain and recovery. Write down everything," he reiterates while looking very pleased with himself.

We drink our coffee, and I leave Ethan's office building still in a bit of a confused state.

*   *   *

When I arrive home, I start writing everything I can think of down on big flip chart sheets and stick them to the walls of my study. As I stand back to read all the phrases and random thoughts posted on the wall, I realize that almost all have something to do with purpose and pain.

I reflect deeply. I read more books. I observe more people. I talk to colleagues, and I start forming a model in my head. Every day, the model crystallizes more and more.

Reflection as a business starts doing well. I employ somebody to take care of all the administration, and I start thinking that I have things going in the right direction at long last. It is during this time that I meet a person who becomes a dear friend and partner in the business.

AJ attends one of the workshops I facilitate at our church. He approaches me with the purpose-question himself. He is unhappy with his current work situation. When I share with him that I plan to write a course with a purpose model as a theme, he volunteers to do the writing, using my inputs.

After AJ joins Reflection, we share many fruitful discussions, excellent brainstorming sessions, and successful product development days. AJ joining forces with me was one of the best days of my life.

Chapter 8 title

CHAPTER 8

The Hellfire

"Can you stand the heat of the fire?" I ask, pausing for dramatic effect. I am in the coaching room with a client, concluding our hour-long session. I look into her eyes, dramatically launching my final remark: "Only if you have character, and you truly, truly know who you are."

The client nods in agreement. "That is so true, Rina."

I am happy to see I have made the right impact when a smile spreads across her face—another satisfied customer.

A few days after this successful session, I receive a disturbing call from one of my most important clients requesting an urgent personal meeting. Robert is not the type of client who would normally visit your office. You usually are required to call on him.

I am still pondering the possible reasons for Robert's request and how to handle it when the receptionist informs me that my visitor has arrived. The meeting doesn't last long, and the message is curt and clear.

"We are unfortunately halting your company's consulting services. Our company needs to cut costs, and we have decided to end our contract with you. All your consultants currently working on projects for us can call it a day. This is with immediate effect." And with a perfunctory greeting, he just gets up and leaves me sitting in my chair—completely speechless.

The words cut through my body like a cold, sharp knife. The blade slices through me in slow motion. It starts as acute pain in my head, disorienting me. The sensation moves down to contract my throat. It grips my heart with ice and sucks the air from my lungs. Nausea rises in my stomach, and my legs start to tremble. I am paralyzed and cold, feeling cut off from the life source. Then very slowly, I feel life creeping back, warm blood flowing and heat returning to my body. I know I am in shock!

I go through the next few days like an automatic robot.

* * *

Luckily, we are busy with another project for a smaller client for which AJ and I need to travel quite a lot. This project helps me avoid the moment when I have to deal with the fact that our biggest client has terminated our contract. The financial implication is devastating for our business. This is what happens when you put all your eggs in one basket! I am so angry with myself.

To try to forget the loss of this essential big contract, I throw myself into my work. We manage to get a minor contract to do a psychometric assessment project for a new client. We spend four months on this assignment and complete it successfully. I have arranged with the suppliers of the assessment material only to pay them on completion of the project. I submit the invoice, rather a hefty one, to the company for the completed assessments. This is going to save us financially.

Almost immediately, I receive a return email. It reads, "The person who authorized this contract did not have the authority to do so. The company does not authorize the work and the payment, and we will therefore not pay the invoice."

The words cut through my body like a cold, sharp knife. The blade slices through me in slow motion, dissecting every part—till my body parts reconnect again. The whole shock response plays out.

My world implodes, and I am at a complete loss. Where to now?

I get hold of my lawyer, and he launches a legal process to try to at least recover some payment for work delivered. I call the suppliers of all the materials and negotiate new payment terms. To my surprise, they accept reasonable down-payment terms. I am so grateful. There are still some good people in this world.

During this tumultuous time, AJ casually strolls into my office one morning and launches into a lengthy monologue, which I barely follow. In my stressed state of mind, the details of the conversation are blurred. However, I somehow agree to buy back his shareholding in the business with the last available funds in the company's bank account. What on earth is happening?

I pray.

I ask God for a sign.

I pray more.

I feel alone.

There is only a deathly silence. Not the slightest sign or indication from God or the Universe to acknowledge my existence at all.

* * *

A friend phones me out of the blue. "We have a new business deal, and we want your company to work on the contract with us. The services you offer are complementary to ours. Are you in?" Marco asks.

"Of course, thank you. We are always in." I try to stay as calm as possible. Is this the lifeline I have been praying for? Has the Universe been listening to me?

Slowly, I manage to rebuild my confidence. The belief in my capability that I have lost through all the previous negative and backbreaking experiences is coming back. Nothing is as humbling as a huge business failure to bring you back to basics and harsh reality.

The business venture with the company where Marco is a senior consultant continues for almost a year. And then, *bang!*

A values difference can create a big void. A business partnership cannot work if the entities are perceived to have different value systems. I feel so strongly about my point of view that I decide to leave. My lawyer makes all the necessary calls and legal arrangements. It is an excruciating process.

I start to question myself and my own values. *What is wrong with me? Why can't I work with other people? Are my values skewed?*

To top it all off, my trusted colleague AJ announces his resignation. He is leaving my company to pursue other avenues. It is a dark day. However, Marco resigns from his company shortly after that and joins me as an associate consultant at Reflection. A good day in return. You lose some; you win some.

*   *   *

Unbelievably, this strange scenario repeats itself three more times. A phone call to join a business venture. We are in. *Bang!* The difference in values rears its ugly head, and we are saved by a lawyer.

The questions continue to swamp me from all sides.

What on earth is wrong with me?

Why can't I manage to work with other people?

Are my values skewed?

Am I a failure?

There is anger at myself because I could not see what was coming. I not only hurt myself, I hurt the people in my business who are standing by me. I hurt my family because they see me go through this pain time and time again. Each business separation is like going through a divorce. A harrowing divorce.

Stop, Rina!

Let's take stock.

I sit at my desk and evaluate my business life. I have a difficult conversation with myself. I have had shock after shock. My lawyer had to bail me out every time. I am emotionally drained to the point where I find my body rejecting certain foods. I go to bed with severe pain every night. These are mostly burning sensations in the pit of my stomach.

Visits to several medical doctors have me taking allopathic medicine every day—probably for the rest of my life. Not to mention the fact that I can barely walk. My health compass, my dystonic foot, is playing up again and warning me of the severe stress my body is under. I barely make it through each new day.

Sitting behind the desk in my office, I want to quit. Give up Reflection Consulting. Things are just not working for me. It feels as if I am in a hellfire. But should it be this difficult? Can things not be easier? I rack my brains to find an answer but can only manage to think something is wrong.

*   *   *

A couple of days later, I am the proverbial early bird at the office again. Sitting behind my computer, I sense the silence in the offices around me. It is so quiet that I can almost hear the blood pumping through my veins.

"Do you really think all these people are against you? Causing this hellfire?" I hear a voice ask.

"What? Who?" I almost look around in my office. But then realize it is not a voice I hear with my ears.

"I repeat, do you really think all these people are against you?" the voice asks again.

"Before I answer this question, who is asking?" I challenge back.

"Rina, this is important for your life going forward. Do you really think all these people are against you?" the voice insists.

"I refuse to answer the question before you tell me, *who are you*?" I adamantly demand.

"No, you tell me, who are you?" the voice challenges back.

It feels as if someone has thrown a bucket of cold water at me. Who am I?

"I am a highly moral person ..."

Am I really?

Am I this highly moral person who judges everybody who crosses my path?

Remember the question to my former consulting client?

"Can you stand the heat of a fire?"

"Only if you have character and you truly, truly know who you are."

I go around asking other people this highly moral question, and I cannot stand the heat myself!

Wait a minute. These business relationship failures were not about a bunch of nasty people trying to get me. Somehow, the heat is turned on, and people are just playing a role. Actually, they are doing me a favor by playing their part. They are getting hurt themselves.

It is like extracting gold from ore. In order to separate the gold from the rock, extreme heat is applied. Through an almost magical alchemical process, pure gold then flows from the ore. I suddenly realize I am not in a hellfire—I am in a heal-fire.

I am purified to a crystal-clear understanding of my mission on earth, but at the same time, my character and identity are refined. I am tested on my declarations of my principles. It is not only about *what* you do but also about *how* you do it.

The heat is turned on to see if pure gold is flowing. I have to stand in my own true power. Breaking others down and blaming them for my failure is not true power. True power is thanking them for my experiences. They are bringing the heat and the alchemy so that the gold can flow. I am in serious identity and character training.

I grab my journal and quickly write this new insight down, ending with a flourish courtesy of Peter Parker's Spiderman principle: "With great power comes great responsibility."

CHAPTER 9

The Toxic Air

As consultants, part of our work is facilitating people and business growth processes. Regarded in the industry as a good facilitator, I can stay objective and distance myself from the unfolding process. This is a very handy skill in my own life as well. It allows me to keep the external process of earning a living as a consultant separate from my internal process of experiencing and reflecting life. Therefore, the struggle of my life journey is never reflected in my professional work. Well, maybe the gold is shining, but never the heat of the melting process.

If I had to share my life story, few people would believe how hard it has been for me. This is because I internalize my own learnings and, subsequently, teach them. And then these ring true. People sense authenticity in my theories without me having to share the details of my life.

It is the same with the team work I am doing today. I look at the team sitting in front of me. I sense their hardships and their pain. Let me give them something to ponder on, to ease their pain. People always say I have the gift of taking complex theories and explaining them in simple ways. I love to use pictures in my presentations. I search on my computer, and the next moment a giant jellyfish wobbles across the big presentation screen.

I start talking. "Life, or what I would like to call the Universe, sends a jellyfish your way to help you deal with something. This jellyfish is usually in the form of a life trauma. You fight with your jellyfish, and then you win. Once you take a step back, you realize your jellyfish experience has taught you a lesson."

I flip to the next slide and read some facts about jellyfish from Wikipedia: "They are typified as free-swimming marine animals consisting of a gelatinous umbrella-shaped bell and trailing tentacles. The bell can pulsate for locomotion, while stinging tentacles can be used to capture prey. Touching or being touched by a jellyfish can be very uncomfortable. Sting effects range from no effect to extreme pain to death. Even beached and dying jellyfish can still sting when touched."

I look at the faces around the conference table. Some are nodding in agreement, and I continue. "When the Universe sends you a huge wobbly trauma jellyfish to fight, it will keep you busy for a while. If you survive, you will learn a wonderful lesson about life."

Carried away, I continue philosophically, "However, after a while, it might dawn on you that the insight from the lesson has a familiar feel to it—as if you recognize the insight from somewhere before but have just forgotten it. Therefore, when you reflect and recover, you will intuitively know it is not a new lesson. You had known it all along."

Somehow, I forget that I am also going to be tested on my fancy theories and dramatic declarations. My first tiny jellyfish arrives in the form of an economy not favoring the business of consulting. It is 2008—the year of worldwide economic collapse. Though we manage to secure a contract with one of our corporate clients, requests for general consultations start to dry up.

Marco—now one of my associates—and I put our heads together and decide that our business needs aggressive marketing. Unfortunately, a small business such as ours does not have the luxury of a marketing unit, or for that matter, a fat budget to spend on advertising. You remain your own best advertisement, as your time is too expensive to fritter away on marketing follies. However, we need some magic, and in a small business, one needs to wear many hats. I start spending more and more time at the office.

As my body wears down, I am almost always tired and tense. I find myself looking forward to weekends more eagerly than ever before. It is Saturday, and I try to relax on a daybed in our living room at home, listlessly paging through a magazine I don't really want to read. The next moment, my teenager Katy breathlessly rushes into the room and says, "Mom, I must get a wax still today. Can you please take me?"

I phone the usual beauty salon—fully booked. As are all the salons near us. Eventually, I manage to get an appointment at a spa not too far away.

On our return from Katy's spa wax, I flop back onto the daybed again. My dear husband is still where I had left him, watching sport from his favorite armchair in front of the TV.

"I think I need to start my own salon," I say.

"I think that is a pretty good idea," he absently replies.

I jump up to fetch my laptop. For the rest of the afternoon, I google everything on salons and spas. I start to draft a business plan with predictions on income and expenses. I have office space available, and it makes so much sense to use that area for a beauty salon.

The next day, my enthusiasm is contagious as I take the Reflection team along on this new journey. Everybody participates by researching organic products and equipment.

We execute the weekend-written business plan within a month in an industry we know nothing about. Soon, I realize that every business and industry has its challenges, and ours is to find therapists. With the high level of unemployment in our country, one would think finding a suitable candidate would be easy. However, it proves a bit trickier than I had planned. But we persevere, and a trained therapist is appointed. We launch what we believe to be a beautiful and tranquil beauty salon.

*   *   *

A week after the launch, excitement levels are still high. But somewhere inside my body, tremors of tension are starting to flare up. Quite soon, I realize that writing a business plan over a weekend and executing it in one month, plus the burden of an enormous financial risk, is taking its toll on my body. At this stage, I wake up at night with my hands totally numb and my stomach a tight nauseous knot. During the day, I suffer from bouts of trembling, and when driving, my left foot, my usual stress indicator, finds it hard to hit the brake. Every morning I wake up covered in a film of sweat.

Fortunately, I have a strong mind, and I file every challenge in the correct box in my head. This disciplined habit never ceases to amaze me. I can take an issue, put it in the right place in my head, and later attend to it for a complete analysis. These internal sessions can keep me busy for hours on end. All the while, my family tries in vain to get through to me.

What works for me is when I can cluster my stress symptoms together in boxes in my head. It makes it easier to analyze, explain, google, and rationalize. So, I cluster all my symptoms of numb hands, waking up at night, and trembling under a mineral deficiency. I take more vitamins and minerals, and, in my head, problem solved. I convince myself that I have done a wellness course, and I know what I am doing.

Some time earlier, I had attended a neuro coaching course. There I learned about the amygdala highjack, which is an immediate and overly emotional response to an actual trigger. Because I know these things, I can surely manage my own emotional stress. So, this problem is also solved.

As far as the hot flashes I experience in the morning, that must be premenopause creeping up on me. And in this organized way of clustering things in boxes, I tell myself that all is well. If I can solve the problems in my head, all have been taken care of.

*   *   *

The beauty salon has been open for a few months now, but things are not looking good. We have not yet managed to establish a solid client base, and the new wellness studio, as we now call it, is struggling. I find it hard to understand. I have always thought consulting to be a challenging career, but I am starting to realize that every industry has its own demands and obstacles.

A small business will always face challenges. These will include paying for marketing and financial services, finding the best employees, and meeting their paycheck expectations. Financial institutions are always hesitant to lend money to small business enterprises, given their high-risk factor. Therefore, it is quite a challenge for me to find a couple of small loans to tide us over. In another unfortunate complication, we underprice our services. The world of the small business entrepreneur is fraught with high stress, risks, worries about attracting clients, and worst of all, the omnipresent crisis of cash flow.

In addition to the stress from the wellness studio, the type of work we do in the consulting area deals with emotionally loaded situations like cultural changes and leadership resistance. On top of that follows the expectation from businesses that we will resolve all their issues and enable performance at the drop of a hat. We like to compare ourselves to a fire department: when everybody runs from the burning building, we run in to repair, restore, restructure, and resolve.

The main characteristic of an entrepreneur is endurance—the same endurance long-distance runners have. They need the ability to keep going even when bone-tired, sick to their stomach, and completely drained emotionally. They have had enough and want to give up but must endure and cross the finish line. It is the same thing in the business world. When working on projects or getting new contracts, endurance is what sets you apart from the pack. You hit the automatic pilot button and keep going—completing the race despite pain or discomfort.

Other essential qualities of successful entrepreneurs are their energy and the ability to do things right now. Not tomorrow or the day after—now! That is because when an opportunity exists, you immediately need to grab it with both hands. You will find yourself working while others sleep. You will be the first to arrive at the office in the morning and the last to leave at night. And to do this, you need energy.

The other characteristic which probably gives me the most trouble because I am a stickler for it, is a sense of precision, otherwise labeled *perfectionism*. When you are working in a small business, there are no second chances. This means you must get things right the first time. Every mistake translates into irritated or dissatisfied clients, loss of money, and eventually loss of business.

One thing people forget to mention when advocating entrepreneurship is the need for an irrational and illogical ability to sacrifice personal needs. Business always comes first. I cannot remember ever coming across this truth when reading books on entrepreneurship. If I had, I probably would not have understood what that would mean in reality.

Since I have become an entrepreneur, I have missed hair and doctor appointments, lunches, and evening theatre outings with family and friends. I have canceled so many coffee dates with my girlfriends that I am not even invited anymore. I have sacrificed evenings, weekends, and holidays with my family—occasions that were meant to be times of rest for me. It feels as if my identity of self has been erased. You become the face of the business. With time being your best asset as a business consultant, you jealously guard it and use it only for business ventures. Because in business, time is money.

The last entrepreneurial characteristic that springs to mind is the ability to make tough and sometimes difficult decisions. Most people will try to give these a wide berth, but in business, it is unavoidable. People did not always take kindly to some of the decisions I had to make as a small entrepreneur. In the bigger corporate world, you can afford to have your employees make mistakes, allow them to take time to develop their skills, and do on-the-job training. That luxury is not available to consulting small businesses in particular. You need to be an expert from day one. Clients want value for their money and expect top-class service. And when you are the boss, that means your try to hire the best, fire them when they don't perform, and end relationships with suppliers who fall short. It is the hardest part of my job, as I must make decisions that impact other people's lives.

I almost forgot the one characteristic that was, and still is, the best part of my job: a passion for nurturing people. I quickly learned that keeping your skills and philosophies to yourself is not to anybody's benefit. We started sharing these and more at Reflection Consulting, and the most wonderful thing happened. Excellent models and methodologies developed, and think tanks expanded. Having both young and experienced people in the company is an added benefit. The concept of a think tank works well, and we make a difference in companies with the things we invent there.

This is my reflection and experience with regards to entrepreneurship and the character of a true entrepreneur. To live up to these expectations and survive the emotional turmoil of trying to be the best entrepreneur possible is my own struggle with my personal jellyfish.

* * *

I am currently wrestling with two separate wobbly blobs of jelly. The consulting firm is in financial dire straits again, and the new wellness studio is not making any money. This is hard to deal with. By now, I even wake up in the middle of the night, and after tossing and turning am wide awake at five in the morning. My hot flashes drive me crazy. I am constantly tired, and my irritation with all and sundry is almost palpable. But one way or another, I push ahead.

My fascination with health and wellness led me to open the wellness studio. It was a huge financial layout, but in my heart, I felt that it was the right thing to do at the time. Now that I think about it, maybe it has something to do with my quest for the *healing* part of my life purpose. I write a note to myself: *Make time to read more about health and wellness.*

And so, over time, I study and explore Western and Eastern perspectives on health and wellness. I get to know all the theories. The bookshelf in my office is stocked to the rafters with the evidence of my research. The authors are the masters of my teaching. My eyes roam over the titles:

- *Wheels of Life* and *Eastern Body Western Mind* by Anodea Judith
- *Science and the Akashic Field* by Ervin László
- *The Tapping Solution* by Nick Ortner
- *Defy Gravity: Healing Beyond the Bounds of Reason* by Caroline Myss
- *The Biology of Belief: Unleashing the Power of Consciousness, Matter and Miracles* by Bruce Lipton
- *Emergence: Seven Steps for Radical Life Change* by Derek Rydall

- *You Can Heal Your Life* by Louise Hay
- *Mind to Matter: The Astonishing Science of How Your Brain Creates Material Reality* by Dawson Church

I have so many theories and answers available to me in all these books. But for whatever reason, I instead choose to wrestle the jellyfish. Why?

*   *   *

Something slowly starts sneaking up on me, at first unnoticed. It begins as an innocent thought. But then I start repeating this thought, completely unaware that it is starting to create a negative thought pattern. And worst of all, I don't realize that it is gathering similar thoughts to keep it company.

Remember Hebb's rule that says, "What fires together, wires together"?

The thoughts crystalize into beliefs. The beliefs assemble into a mind-state system. The mind-state system becomes my absolute truth, which informs my life attitude and every decision I make. I associate so strongly with this negative, toxic mind state, I become depressed. Every word that leaves my mouth is negative. Everything I need to do is an effort, and I let everybody around me know that it is. I find fault with everything that people around me do.

Every day, I sink deeper and deeper into this downward spiral of a depressed mind state. I feel useless and worthless, and the more I feel like this, the more I treat others like this. I treat them as if they are useless and worthless objects. I project my pain onto others.

My attitude becomes so toxic that my key employee, my right hand at Reflection Consulting, decides to leave. Others follow. My heart aches.

Depression pulls me into a dark pit from which there seems to be no escape. I cry at the office. I cry at home. I cry behind my computer during the day. I cry in my bed at night. An enormous sadness has wrapped its tentacles around my heart. Hubby tries to break through the dark mist, but I have convinced myself that I am a failure. I am alone. The journey I am on just stretches endlessly like a train on a track to nowhere, hurtling forward.

The bleak crisis reaches its climax one morning. I am driving on the main highway between Pretoria and Johannesburg on my way to meet a client. Without thinking, I start to accelerate. I watch the speedometer climbing. A calmness settles over me. It will be easy. Just flick the steering wheel to the side. Nobody will know. It will look like an accident. My heart pounds in my head. It is easy. *Go faster!* My foot hits the gas. *Faster!* A quick flick to the side.

Nobody will know. It will look like an accident.

The easy way out. I go faster.

But I am dearly loved …

"You will not do it!" commands the voice.

"You again?" I ask as tears stream down my face.

"You need help!" says the voice.

"Help! Who will help me? Nobody can help me," I scream.

"There is always help. You are choosing to ignore it. Do you really believe the Universe wants to punish you like this? Your ego is your biggest enemy. Just because you have a smart brain does not mean you know it all. As a matter of fact, you know nothing. Pull yourself together, meet your client, and then phone the doctor to help you," the stern voice booms.

"Which doctor?" I ask in a daze.

"Now *really*." The voice gives an exasperated sigh, then adds in a more sympathetic tone, "The doctor your friend recommended last week."

On return from the meeting in Johannesburg, I pull into the parking bay at my office, a numbness in my arms on the steering wheel. Although the meeting went well, I have no recollection of what was discussed or agreed on. I physically feel my heart pounding against my rib cage. My breath is shallow. The jellyfish is literally squeezing the air from my lungs. I gather the meeting was successful, as there is a message from the client on my phone. They want to proceed with their session and request Reflection to facilitate.

I rummage around in my handbag and, by some miracle, find the details of the medical practitioner my friend had recommended scribbled on a piece of scrap paper. I call the doctor's rooms and manage to secure an urgent appointment.

Still sitting in my car, unable to make an effort to go to my office, I place another critical call. This time to Heaven.

"Please take Reflection back. I have had it with this company! It is over. I am not fit for this job. If I carry on with this business, I am going to die. Reflection is killing me. I resign!"

*   *   *

The subsequent journey of physical healing after my diagnosed burnout takes a while. Luckily, this specific general practitioner also specializes in integrative medicine, and she helps me make healthy natural choices. Under her guidance, I manage to lower my dangerously high blood pressure without allopathic, chemical medicine. I have a strong head and will. Once I put my mind to it, I can make it work. I choose no alcohol, no caffeine, healthy food, and exercise. Slowly, I start feeling the air and breath of life coming back into my lungs. The jellyfish is losing its grip.

I lose the wellness studio because there just isn't enough cash flow to carry it. It feels like losing a child. So much went into giving it life, and now it is gone. Packing up the last of the equipment to give away, my tears fall into the cardboard boxes as well. The loneliness is all over me. I am sad and alone. And still, my purpose escapes me. Whom to heal? How to heal?

A financial lifebuoy comes my way by means of a change-management project for a client at their premises in Johannesburg. For the next eight months, I do a daily commute from Pretoria by express train to run their program. I work with an incredible team of young change managers, and I enjoy sharing my knowledge with them. Unbeknown to them, the Universe grants me these eight months to heal and recover.

During this time, while still working in Johannesburg, I wake up one morning with the word *surrender* echoing in my head. Climbing the stairs at the train station for my early-morning commute, a silent conversation starts inside me.

"Surrender," the voice says.

"Surrender what?" I ask.

"Surrender your ego," the voice replies.

"Excuse me. I lost the salon. I lost almost everything. The consulting company is barely surviving. I am holding on by the skin of my teeth, keeping it afloat for the few people who still earn their living there. Did I not hand Reflection back that terrible day in the parking lot? Go away!" I say angrily.

"Surrender your ego, not your company," the voice says.

"I lose both my company and my wellness studio, and literally everybody from family to friends to clients knows about it. The whole industry knows it! I am standing with my back against the wall. Ego? Where is the ego? Leave me alone!" I scream silently.

"Surrender your ego. Otherwise, you cannot forgive every person who has ever hurt or left you alone," the voice says.

"They hurt and left me!" It is an outcry to the Universe!

A fellow commuter behind me almost bumps into me as I come to a complete stop on the stairs going down to the trains. I mumble a hurried apology, still confused by the conversation rattling in my head.

"Exactly. Who wants to be around an egoistic, unforgiving fool? Surrender your ego and forgive them." The voice is equally determined now.

"Go …," but before I can complete my sentence, I sense the voice is gone. No use then for further conversation, with only strangers and cold concrete stairs around me. The rest of the day is one hard struggle, trying to concentrate and keeping my professional pose at the office.

*   *   *

For a few years now, I have noticed my weird relationship with books. By some strange coincidence, books with answers to my existential life questions seem to veer my way. Don't know how, don't know why. It is almost like the mythical character in the *Thor* movies. When in danger, he holds out his hand, and a huge iron hammer flies into it. With this powerful tool, he can overcome any crisis. My powerful hammer flies to me in the form of books.

I will hold my hand out by asking a question. Then the book will appear, sometimes in the strangest ways. Once, when I was attending a course, the woman sitting opposite me reached across the conference table and scribbled the title and author of a book on my notepad. As my teenager would say, "That's random!" Random indeed. This woman did not even know me. Neither had I asked a question nor given any indication that I needed this information from her.

The books find me through Hubby's hands, friends' recommendations, emails from contacts, and social media in general. I know immediately when I should pay attention to special books. This magically happened the first time in high school, when Daleen Matthee's *Circles in a Forest* landed on my desk. And the Universe continues to send these precious gifts to me. So now there is a huge library with hundreds of books in my house and an ever-growing collection of e-books on my Kindle.

I recall two almost surreal incidents involving books finding their way to me. The first was a book received in the mail. I cannot recall ever ordering the book, but it arrived, neatly addressed to me in person. It was posted in the United States and ended up in my mailbox in South Africa. How, I still don't know.

The second incident came about because of a coaching client who was severely traumatized and possibly on the verge of committing suicide. At the time, I was working on a proposal for a corporate client. Sitting in front of my computer, I suddenly felt the urge to fetch a specific book from my library upstairs. Usually, I am too lazy to do that, as it is a steep climb up a set of narrow winding steel stairs. However, that day, I had no problem. Book in hand, I opened it to read a particular page. I must add that this book had nothing to do with the project I was working on at the time.

While I was still engrossed in the book, wondering why the page was important, my office assistant called with an urgent message to contact the distressed coaching client. The words on that page were my guidance to a desperate and broken man in his time of need.

I often find that a particular message is meant for other people. Many times, I will read a book and, within days, a friend or client will have a question for me. And lo and behold, I have a ready answer!

Of course, I overlooked this gift from the Universe at first. Luckily, as my awareness grew, I started noticing the book magic. I often joke about this, saying that the Universe knows I will read the books. Therefore, the Universe is using this way to communicate with me. It is like emails from heaven.

By now, I know how to work the book magic.

Ask the question and wait for the answer.

So, it is at this point in my duel with the Universe about my ego that I revert to my tried and trusted book magic trick. "How on earth must I surrender my ego?" I ask and let the question hang in the air. I do not have to wait for long. *A New Earth: Awakening to Your Life's Purpose* by Eckhart Tolle finds me. When the learner is ready, the teacher will rise.

I eagerly read: "Underneath the surface appearance, everything is not only connected with everything else, but also with the Source of all life out of which it came. Even a stone, flower and bird, could show you the way back to God, to the Source, to yourself."

I sit back and reflect on this for a moment. It is aligned with what Ervin László said, "consciousness evolution is from the ego-bound to the transpersonal form." There is a collective consciousness, an akasha.

I continue to read from Tolle:

> The word "I" embodies the greatest error and the deepest truth, depending on how it is used. In conventional usage, it is not only one of the most frequently used words in the language but also one of the most misleading. In normal everyday usage, "I" embodies the primordial error, a misperception of who we are, an illusory sense of identity. This is the ego. This illusory sense of self is what Albert Einstein referred to as an optical illusion of consciousness. That illusory self then becomes the basis for all further interpretations or rather misinterpretations of

> reality, all thought processes interactions, and relationships. Your reality becomes a reflection of the original illusion. If you can recognize illusion as illusion, it dissolves.

I sit back. So we are never alone. We are always connected. Every time pain is inflicted somewhere in the system, everybody feels it. The impact of these words almost takes my breath away.

Dying to Be Me by Anita Moorjani also finds me. Her message is very simple:

> I don't have to try to live up to other people's expectations of perfection and then feel inadequate when I fail miserably. I am at my most powerful when I allow myself to be who life intended me to be. I am at my most powerful when I am working with life rather than against it. When we are aware of our own magnificence, we don't feel the need to control others and we don't allow ourselves to be controlled.

It all comes together in these words that echo within me too: "The recognition of I am love, allows me to release all fear and all judgment."

I think I am beginning to understand what it means to surrender your ego. But it is only when *The Seat of the Soul* by Gary Zukav finds me that the forgiveness part really starts making sense:

> Forgiveness means that you do not hold others responsible for your experiences. If you do not hold yourself accountable for what you experience, you will hold someone else accountable, and if you are not satisfied with what you experience, you will seek to change it by manipulating that person. When you hold someone responsible for what you experience,

you lose power. You cannot know what another person will do. Therefore, when you depend on another person for the experiences that you think are necessary to your well-being, you live continually in the fear that they will not deliver. The perception that someone else is responsible for what you experience underlies the idea that forgiveness is something that one person does for the other. How can you forgive another person for the fact that you have chosen to step out of your power? When you forgive, you release critical judgment of yourself as well as for others. You lighten up. You do not cling to negative experiences that resulted from decisions that you made while you were learning. Regret works the same. Do you regret your learning experience?

Deducting then from this, I should be grateful to the people who were willing to play a role in all my life experiences. Then there is really nothing to forgive. I chose my own suffocating jellyfish. I chose the experiences. The people were willing role players in my experiences. Some of them were very dear to me, and they themselves were hurt in the process. I can only hope their life journeys will also allow them to find this truth and healing.

It is the truth that sets you free. Though I must add as an aside, "The truth will set you free, but first, it will piss you off."

If then I don't have to forgive anybody, and everybody I meet is playing a willing part in experiences I have chosen, all that remains is love and gratitude. Only people who love me deeply agreed to be part of my soul's growth. Imagine the sacrifice of agreeing to be the villain in somebody's life story. Therefore, I am genuinely grateful to all, as well as for my experiences of growth.

When we miss the realization of how our experiences unfold and the role of others in our growth, the air within and around us becomes toxic with our hate, judgment, and revenge. However, when we grasp this, we become the true love we are supposed to be. Only then can we radiate the air with love. Then we have the breath of life.

CHAPTER 10

The False Beat

Near the end of 2018, sitting at the large oak desk in my office, I stare at my life journal with unseeing eyes. As always, colored pens are handy to jot down my insights into the world of Self. It is still early morning, and I am the first one at the office as usual. I love these quiet times I spend with my journal reflecting on the meaning and purpose of life. My mind dwells back on the past three years, and I begin to write.

When you give something back to the Universe, the Universe will take it back. I write these words in big, bold red letters and then continue writing the rest of the story as it plays in my mind using a dark green pen.

Toward 2016, Reflection as a consulting business had reached a dead end. Some of my associate consultants were allowed to continue working on a couple of contracts. However, it was my intention to let the contracts run their course and then to close Reflection when these ended. After all, I had given Reflection back to the Universe in the parking lot!

Despite my best and most earnest efforts, the consulting did not work, and I was the first to acknowledge it. I had failed. There were some good times too, but it was all over. It was final. I was going to do freelance consulting in the future.

Following the end of the road for Reflection, I started looking for new projects and then got the assignment in Johannesburg. That project has always been what I refer to as my sabbatical year. There was time to slow down, earn a stable income, and best of all, invest in my health.

But toward the end of my so-called sabbatical year, the restlessness started again.

"Why are you downcast, O my soul? Why so disturbed within me?"

This restlessness made it easy to say yes when I was asked to join forces with another consulting company. I had never actually closed Reflection completely. This merger was a wonderful way out of the doldrums, and I was extremely excited. My initial thought was that, at long last, I would get the opportunity to be part of a successful consulting company. The two different consulting houses consolidated, and together we dreamed of a bright, prosperous future.

This was my third business marriage. I was of the belief that the merger was the key to the castle. Unfortunately, the honeymoon phase was short-lived, and soon, the partners were in conflict.

* * *

At that point, it was time for Hubby to run his yearly marathon in Kaapsehoop, a beautiful and tranquil small town set high in the misty mountains of Mpumalanga province in South Africa. The town is well known for herds of wild horses freely roaming around in the surrounding area.

Early on the morning of the race, white ghostlike fingers of fog still sweeping across the valley, I was sitting in our car. The race was about to start a few miles away, and I was to watch the runners as they passed.

The next moment, I saw them: not the runners but a small family of horses crossing the road right in front of me. A beautiful golden-brown mare was leading the way, closely followed by a tiny caramel-colored foal. At the rear was a big, fierce-looking black stallion. It was almost magical to be so close to these majestic wild animals.

Still slightly lightheaded from what I had witnessed, I felt a realization jolt through me. The business marriage I found myself in was like trying to tame a wild horse.

Unfortunately, it had been like a wild horse from the start. It was a horse I just could not tame, no matter how hard I tried. At that stage, the new business was leaving me feeling mentally and physically drained.

Watching the last of the mist swirl away down the road, I had a revelation. I decided to walk away. The wild horses symbolized what I needed to do to be free.

This last business venture had lasted for just over a year. That was probably too short a time to really be a success, and it felt weird to scuttle it. Maybe the Universe had other ideas, and I misread the message. But I just could not make any sense of it.

* * *

There was a price to be paid for leaving, and I had to pay with my health again. The first clue that I was in a bad business marriage had been when I was diagnosed with shingles. The left side of my face was in agony, and the constant pain was almost unbearable. The stress of trying to be the mediator between the business partners was proving to be too much for my body to handle.

In retrospect, from where I am now, I have to admit that I was not doing well as a self-appointed mediator. If I am completely honest, I made a real mess of things.

Shingles is a condition brought on by stress. At some point, the doctor feared that I would lose my left eye or the hearing in my left ear. The correct medication and care luckily prevented this. The only side effect I am left with today is an intermittent nerve contraction of my tongue. When tired or stressed, my tongue will produce a hissing snakelike sound. Embarrassingly, I sometimes sound like I have had one too many!

At this point, I sit back in my chair and look at the story I have just written in my journal. It needs a conclusion. If I am honest, I think I have not been truthful to myself, to who I really am. I was so occupied with keeping the partners calm and happy that I forgot to be the real and true Rina.

"If you dim your light, you are not doing the world a favor," I say out loud. "And once again, you had to pay the price," I add in a whisper.

The long and the short of it is that we went through a cold and impersonal business divorce. Leaving was not the worst of it—I lost a few valuable collegial friends in the process. It was one of those situations where you know there will always be professional respect, but you will never be friends again.

I am truly sorry that I lost you all, I write in the journal.

I look at the pen in my hand. I have always had this quirky habit of using different color pens for journaling. I put the green pen back in the holder and look to pick a new color for the next story. It is as if I have finished a chapter and what is to follow is a new beginning. I choose a bright red pen for the next chapter.

*   *   *

I was still reeling from the previous business venture coming to its abrupt end and probably not thinking straight, but I immediately fell in love again, with a business marriage following soon thereafter, my fourth of its kind. A year later, another business divorce. This time I was really devastated, losing friends so close, they were almost like family.

This last red paragraph looks like a wound on the paper. That is exactly what I feel like at the time: wounded. To write the conclusion to these painful business experiences, I need to find some peace. And choose a turquoise blue pen, one of my favorite colors.

I start writing. The last two failed business experiences were bizarre, and I suffered a great deal in the process. The shingles that attacked my throat, tongue, ear, and eyes were the last straw. I suddenly realize something. I ask myself, *What are you not saying? What are you not hearing? What are you not seeing?* I write these three questions in my journal, lest I forget. Now I need answers.

The negative experiences I suffered are starting to make some sense. I was an electric guitar trying to play in a symphony orchestra, an instrument that did not fit in. No matter how well I played, I was out of place. I tried playing softer and softer, hoping my sound would blend in, but it did not. Colleagues unsuccessfully tried to tune and correct me. It ended with me not being able to hear, see, or speak well enough to be part of the orchestra.

The last two business divorces were painful. Divorce is always painful. It goes hand in hand with feelings of rejection, failure, low confidence, and mistrust. I hate those feelings! I pause writing for a moment as all those awful emotions rear their ugly heads again. A couple of deep breaths, and I am brave enough to continue.

But as I keep writing, something strange happens. Normally, I will reflect on the lesson I have learned in such traumatic incidents, but now I feel distant from these two events. It feels as if this time, I was an actor playing a role, just going along for the ride.

My turquoise pen is flying across the page now. The words are tumbling out, and I don't want to lose the truth that is suddenly surfacing. My conclusion is that this journey was theirs, not mine. I was only the instrument in their life growth. Why I felt this way, I could not explain at first.

Immediately, it feels as if something has cleared. It is like fog disappearing in the presence of bright sunlight. An indescribable state of peace fills me. Karma is not something I necessarily believe in, but a thought keeps repeating in my head: *You have cleared and paid your debts.*

An overwhelming sense of sorrow for my former partners fills me. I know they went through pain, and I hope they will one day understand that I was instrumental in their growth journey.

Looking up from my writing, I see the purple-blueish contours of distant hills through my office window. Staring with unseeing eyes, I wonder to myself: *Did I also learn something from these experiences? Or was it mainly so others could learn from it? Or did it happen so I could pay my debts?* Shaking my head because the answer still eludes me, I return to my trusted journal.

Maybe what I learned is what I should not do. I should not lose myself. My instrument is unique and not part of a particular orchestra. I've learned to hear better, see better, and feel the vibrations better now. I can hear my own voice better now, and I can follow my destined path and speak my truth.

The next moment, my hand and pen fly over the page, and I write an entire paragraph without pause or hesitation. It happens so quickly that I have to read it a couple of times before I grasp the full meaning.

The bottom line is that the Universe will use seemingly ordinary and unrelated events to transform people's awareness to higher consciousness. It always works with an orchestrated plan. When I gave Reflection back, I thought it was the end of that road. However, it was transformed and returned to me. I did not recognize it at first. I thought I was now sitting with Mind Matters Consulting, a new tamed horse. But it was Reflection, and the game was upped. I now was managing a free-running wild horse.

Luckily, the Universe prepares us to run with wild horses. It is not for no reason that Jeremiah 12:5 implies: *If you can't run with ordinary people, how can you run with horses?* All people long to live their best life—to combine freedom and ease with purpose and meaning.

CHAPTER 11

A Life Vision

... and then the penny drops!

The anecdote is that Einstein would sit in a relaxed state, holding a penny in his hands. His mind would be in an alpha state—as if falling asleep, but with his subconscious at its most creative. And then, just before he actually fell asleep, the penny would drop from his relaxed hands and bring him back to the present, refreshed and full of creative ideas.

Alpha state is when we access the subconscious with heightened focus and intensity. In beta state, the human mind is at its best to perform normal work or chores. Einstein might even have been in theta state (deep sleep) on occasion! But in alpha state, he could solve mathematical and other challenges—until the penny dropped from his hands to bring him back to the real world.

Why am I thinking of pennies dropping today? That's a good question. Maybe it is just a random thought. It is now early 2019. I don't hear any pennies dropping. My life is so compartmentalized at the moment—each facet in a different box.

The personal growth box is possibly maturing. I have managed to figure out how people have played a huge role in some of my valuable life experiences, something for which I am genuinely grateful.

With regard to the purpose box and the consulting business box, well, I figure both have something to do with *healing*. I know healing should be part of the work I do. It should be part of the consulting. The jigsaw puzzle is, however, still missing a few pieces.

During my last business partnership, which also did not work out well, we started operating under a new business name, Mind Matters Consulting—ironically, with a diamond as the logo. Though the partners left, I stayed on and now continue with the consulting side of the business. In retrospect, it is just Reflection with a new brand, as mentioned earlier.

We are doing more or less the same work as before. But something seems different; I just can't put my finger on it. The business is operating on a different level. We are taking on bigger projects and designing exciting new products. We have upped our game, and I detect a new passion and drive. Yes, something is definitely different.

Suddenly, I feel comfortable in my business again. All the former associate consultants have returned, and we are blessed with a stable workload. Financially it is going well—we are laughing all the way to the proverbial bank. Business is booming.

But, *Why are you downcast, O my soul? Why so disturbed within me?* The restless yearning of my soul is back. I am not seeing any pennies drop at the moment.

Is it my imagination, or can I detect a subtle guidance present? Almost as if a hand is gently guiding me away from certain issues but allowing others into my life, guiding me toward what I don't know yet. The feeling of gentle guidance is more pressing each day.

The guidance makes itself known through my emotions. These become my compass in my daily life. If I make a good decision, I immediately experience feelings of happiness and progress. The moment a wrong decision occurs, I feel utter frustration and resentment. And best of all, when I ask a question, the right books immediately find their way to me.

Interesting, mysteriously interesting.

I even start making jokes about this phenomenon with my colleagues. "The Universe got my back," I throw over my shoulder, leaving the office one day. The next eBook to appear on my Amazon Kindle recommendation list is *The Universe Has Your Back: Transform Fear to Faith* by Gabrielle Bernstein.

Curious and more curious.

*   *   *

With all going well businesswise, I decide I need some fun in my life and enroll in a Reiki course. I find the course most exciting until the day the Reiki instructor looks at me and casually asks, "Tell me more about your foot and the car accident."

I share the details as nonchalantly as I can but quickly realize that she is not letting me off the hook that easily. "What was the lesson from the accident?" she asks.

"I don't know. My life was so rushed and traumatic at that stage. Maybe it happened to slow me down. Maybe I needed to learn to accept things and trust the flow of life," I reply.

"Can you remember what happened right before the accident?" she asks.

I silently mull over this question a bit. I do remember the accident almost in detail, but I have never before tried to recall the events preceding it.

"Well, I was on my way to the editor of my doctoral thesis. It was almost finished and ready to be published," I say, thinking back to that fateful day.

"So, what is holding you back at the moment? What are you afraid to finish or publish now?" she asks.

I am flustered, "What do you mean?"

"Is there a book you want to write or want to finish?" she keeps prodding.

"Well, I guess you can say there is something. I am writing my life story, and I am still contemplating if I should publish it."

"Why don't you finish writing it?" she asks. "What are you afraid of? Are you afraid of success?"

I am stumped for an answer.

For a moment, I am thrown off-balance by her remarks. I have never thought of it this way. Could there really be some subtle resistance keeping me from success? I am aware that I am reluctant to finish this life story. But I am not quite sure what I am so scared of. Aren't all first-time authors scared? I would think that is normal. But it is a bit rich to suggest that I fear success. That is something completely new to me, and I am not sure I like it.

"Can I read you something?" she asks suddenly.

Slowly returning my attention to her, I try to hold myself together, nonchalantly saying, "Yes, of course."

She starts reading a quote from a red-covered book on her coffee table.

Our deepest fear, by Marianne Williamson

Our deepest fear is not that we are inadequate.
Our deepest fear is that we are powerful beyond measure.
It is our light, not our darkness,
that most frightens us.

We ask ourselves,
Who am I to be brilliant, gorgeous, talented, fabulous?
Actually, who are you *not* to be?
You are a child of God.

Your playing small
doesn't serve the world.
There's nothing enlightened about shrinking
so that other people won't feel insecure around you.

We are all meant to shine,
as children do.
We were born to make manifest
the glory of God that is within us.

It's not just in some of us;
it's in everyone.

And as we let our own light shine,
we unconsciously give other people permission
to do the same.
As we're liberated from our own fear,
our presence automatically liberates others.

For a few moments, I stare at her, almost in a daze. This is my truth! For the past fifteen years, I have been recording every life lesson thrown at me, in business as well as personally. But now, I am too afraid to finish and publish this as a book. I have this inherent fear of sharing the *true* story, *my* pain, with the world out there.

A colleague once said, "If only I can get hold of that mysterious journal of yours. We know everything you teach us is written in there. It would make for interesting reading if we could only manage a peek!"

In all the years I have been keeping this journal, I have never shown it to anybody—not my husband or my daughter, not a friend or a colleague. I have used the original notes and rewritten these as a readable book, but nobody has ever seen the result.

I have, however, over time been teaching these concepts and ideas to clients and my colleagues. Yes, I know I am afraid. The

Reiki instructor's insight is exactly the message I need to hear. But I did not expect having to face my demons today.

"A publisher once phoned me," I reluctantly tell her, "but I declined the offer." When I mention the name of the publisher, she stares at me, mouth open in total disbelief.

"You are not serious!" she says. Shaking her head, twirling around, she almost loses her balance but manages to grab the kitchen counter. Following our session, we are busy making herbal tea in the small kitchenette adjacent to her treatment room.

From here on, the rest of the afternoon dissolves into a haze of fragmentary images. The kettle boils; tea is made. She hands me a beautiful green Japanese cup of fragrant tea. Over a small wisp of steam, I look her straight in the eye. I detect a glint in hers—tears, or maybe just light reflecting through the big glass windows of her studio?

It is an awkward moment, but a moment of great truth for me. I suddenly realize the big mistake I made not pursuing the offer from the publisher. My own fear was keeping me from publishing my life story.

I quickly finish my tea, and though she politely tries to make more small talk, I just want to leave as quickly as possible. I need to be alone with my discovery, with the flame that was lit inside me.

I drive home from the Reiki class in a state of euphoria. I must complete the book and publish it. The messages could not be more explicit.

Unfortunately, life has a way of keeping me otherwise occupied. Maybe this time, the forces are working against the Universe. It seems the forces want to prevent some good news from going out into the world. These hostile forces spread the illusion of isolation and aloneness. And I fall into their trap for a while.

But then a gentle hand again brings guidance. It softly nudges me in the desired direction of the Universe that supports the good in the world. The message of hope needs to be out there!

* * *

It is now two months after the Reiki experience, and a friend urges me to try something exciting again. I always enjoy investigating different modalities that tell you more about yourself. As a psychologist and with psychometric assessments being part of my trade, I love exploring these fields.

My friend, knowing my curiosity, recommends an astrological reading. It sounds intriguing, and I jump right in. The Universe is also entertained by enjoyment and excitement.

On many occasions in the past, I have wondered if the "healing" in my purpose had not perhaps been to become a medical doctor. It had been one of the options I considered when deciding on tertiary studies after school. Studying homeopathy was also in the cards at some stage. However, what *healing* meant and *where* and *how* I should live it has always remained the big question.

Nevertheless, I make an appointment with the recommended astrologer for a Skype call in the late afternoon. I know I will be alone at the office then, and I am excited about what will come of this session. I like to think of the Reiki instructor and the astrologer as teachers, crossing my path to teach me, bring me enlightenment.

When the call from the astrologer comes through, she first explains the astrological chart and then starts to ask me several random questions. About twenty minutes into the session, she sends a projectile my way that almost knocks me sideways.

"What do you think is your purpose?" she asks.

"Well, I know it has to do with healing, but I am struggling to find out what that means and how I should go about it," I blurt out. At least this time, I am a bit more prepared to answer these weird questions about my inner self.

"No, it is not that unclear. You should not be a medical doctor or something. You should heal through teaching," she says calmly.

I look at her, a bit skeptical. She has been talking to me for less than half an hour; how can she be so accurate about my life? "Healing through teaching," I smile and continue. "That is a short and very direct conclusion."

She nods. "Yes. It is evident from your astrological chart." And then she slowly repeats, as if I need to absorb it, "Healing through teaching."

"I can live with that," I respond. "As a matter of fact, teaching is exactly what I do in my consulting business. I teach people many different things. And hopefully, empower them to grow and heal."

The text verse I received from Matthew, "Heal the sick," suddenly makes a lot more sense. It is as if the last pieces of the jigsaw puzzle that I have been seeking for so long have just fallen into place. Is this my penny dropping?

The astrologer is not done yet. "I am so glad it is making sense to you. But there is more. Something really creative."

I realize where this is leading and ask with an impish smile, "Something creative like writing a book?"

Giving me a quizzical look, she says, "Yes. According to the chart, something you should finish and send into the world. If this is a book, you should complete and publish it. It is meant to be out in the world, and the time to do it is now."

Well, this is new information. The time for it is now! This is where the penny finally drops for me, and it wakes me from a lifelong sleep. Just to make sure that I have heard her message loud and clear, the astrologer then ties it all together.

"Your purpose is healing through teaching. You should teach through all means available to you, including your creative writing. And the message is clear: the writing must go out now. You will heal others through this book. It is all part of your purpose."

What did Einstein do when his aha moments happened—that moment when the answer jumps at you like a frog from a water lily in a small pond? Did Einstein hear his penny drop and then rushed off to tell somebody of his discovery? Well, this was my penny-drop moment.

The astrologer makes it sound so easy, as if I was supposed to have connected the dots myself. So simple:

Healing through teaching.

Teaching through writing.

Heal the sick.

Why are we not issued manuals at birth? Imagine if the above was the inscription in mine. And with the added instruction that Rina is fragile, and you should treat her gently. Notice her potential and instructions on what else she will need on her path through life. Why don't we have life manuals?

I have one more question for my teacher-astrologer: "I need to know something more. I have had a tough life so far. Is there perhaps a specific reason why?"

She looks at me with genuine compassion and says, "Well, how can you teach if you have not experienced these things firsthand? You can talk with knowledge from your own experience. I will go as far as to say that you contracted and arranged these incidents before your birth."

"I did? Bloody hell!" The swear words slip out before I can stop myself.

Carefully she adds, "The chances are real that you did." She shares a few more ideas with me, and we end the session, her warm, soothing voice still echoing in my ears as the screen fades out.

*   *   *

I am still staring at the blank screen when I think I hear somebody laughing.

"Are you here?" I whisper.

"And how long did that take you?" says the voice.

And with that, the following conversation starts.

"Oh, it is you laughing," I say.

"Do you know how long it took for your penny to drop?" the voice asks.

It might be my imagination, but I think I almost hear a little hidden amusement. I pretend not to notice and start calculating. "It is now 2019. I guess it took me from when my dad passed away in 1999. Is that possible ... that it took me twenty years to figure out my own purpose?" A complete silence descends in the room, as if both the voice and I need to digest the enormity of this fact.

"Oh, by the way, that is only half of the story," the voice says, breaking the silence.

I have no idea where this is leading.

"Go back to your journal again and reread all the life lessons. You will see there is an order and pattern to it. At the moment, you only understand half of your mission," the voice adds.

I am dumbstruck.

Before I can get more details, my office door opens, and a colleague peeps in. I thought everyone had gone home already.

"Are you done with your Skype call?" Thea asks.

"Yes, about ten minutes ago," I answer.

"Oh, I heard you still talking to somebody," she says with a frown.

"I was. I was having a very interesting conversation with myself," I say while smiling, a little embarrassed. "Don't we all do that sometimes?"

"You are so right! By the looks of it, though, it was a rather serious conversation," she says, half laughing.

"Don't worry. My alter ego is just playing up today. Anyway, is there something I can help you with?" I intentionally steer the conversation in a different direction.

When Thea leaves, I lean back in my chair and stare into space. Why is it such a struggle to express our true self to the world? Why are we so afraid to live our purpose, be creative with it, and speak our own truths? I make a mental note to jot this down in my journal as soon as I get home.

The same with the life lessons, of which I apparently must still figure out the pattern. Now that I know that my purpose is to write down my life lessons, I also must find out what else to write down. The holy grail seems to be the pattern of the life lessons. Where is this all to end?

At least for now, I gather that we should express our true self to the world. We should not be afraid to use our creativity to express our purpose and essence. This message had come to me from two different people in the past few months. Both these teachers taught me this valuable and important lesson.

I must admit that I have noticed the life lessons for quite some time now. What intrigues me even more is how I am to find the pattern these lessons had. It is going to take some time to figure that one out!

While gathering my belongings to go home, a thought suddenly strikes me. All the life lessons before this last one came about through trauma and hardship. *Why not this time? I wonder.*

CHAPTER 12

A Different Angle

"When you look at this picture, what do you see?" I ask while showing the well-known illusion of the old lady and the young lady to the audience. I am facilitating a session for one of the leadership teams of a client.

The answers from the audience reflect a typical pattern of some seeing the old lady and some seeing the young lady. It all depends on their focus. I point this psychological phenomenon out to the team. "Depending on where you focus, you will see either. So, when you move your focus, you will see the other one," I explain.

There are a few murmurs and amused giggles in the audience as they help one another see the one or the other. I hear some *aha*s as I move around the training venue, assisting some in the audience with the exercise.

Then I stop dead in my tracks. I have just remembered something. I will have some work to do when I get home!

*   *   *

Back home, I relive my own aha moment from this morning's session. I suddenly know how to look for a pattern in my life lessons. Using pens in different colors to write in my journal is the key. I do the same in other areas of my work too. While I page through my journal, words echo in my head:

Depending on my focus, I will see …

"What will I see?" I ask myself.

"I will see the pattern," the answer comes.

For the past more than twenty years, I have focused on my trauma and learning from the trauma. I must have done a good job, because I know what the life lesson is from each incident. But the pattern is eluding me! I need to find the pattern, but nothing has come to me yet.

Depending on my focus …

I keep paging back and forth in the journal, the various colored paragraphs jumping at me from the pages. Where is the pattern?

Hang on! Very slowly, something starts to emerge. Years of training in psycho-neuro coaching is suddenly paying off. I begin to see a stress response pattern emerging from the different traumas: every time I experience trauma in my life, my brain perceives it as a threat.

The amygdala is a small almond-shaped structure in the brain, essential for our ability to feel certain emotions and to perceive such in other people. These emotions relate to danger, threats, or fear. One could say the amygdala is the alarm center of the body, as it seems to regulate all our reactions to events that are important for our survival.

Once the brain acknowledges a threat, a whole chain of events will follow. The amygdala alerts the hypothalamus, which in turn activates hormones that activate the adrenal glands to secrete adrenaline. The latter activates the body to either fight or flee from danger.

When the threat is not removed, cortisol is released into the body, resulting in more stress, and the amygdala continues to sound the alarm.

Then the focus of the threat will shift from an external stressor to an internal stressor, your own body. However, the body cannot handle constant stress and high levels of cortisol and subsequently collapses.

That explains why I ended up with so many health-related issues and was diagnosed with burnout, depression, or whatever the medical profession calls it.

Depression not being all of it I know from psychoneuroimmunology training. The body releases cytokines that regulate various inflammatory responses. When the production of certain cytokines is overstimulated, it will result in long-term inflammation and an impaired immune system.

There is a clear link between our state of mind and the activation of the stress responses. The mind state can activate the release and suppression of certain brain chemicals. This impacts on the immune system and may cause serious illness. Some experts claim that as much as 80 percent of all illnesses are caused by inflammation.

I rethink the whole process again. If I analyze my own situation, every time I experience a threat, my body responds with its now familiar pattern:

> *The words cut through my body like a cold, sharp knife. The blade slices through me in slow motion. It starts as acute pain in my head, disorienting me. The sensation moves down to contract my throat. It grips my heart with ice and sucks the air from my lungs. Nausea rises in my stomach, and my legs start to tremble. I am paralyzed and cold, feeling cut off from the life source. Then very slowly, I feel life creeping back, warm blood*

flowing, and heat returning to my body. Is this what shock feels like?

I go through the next few days like an automatic robot.

This is my alarm response! This is clearly how I activate my own amygdala and manage to flood my body with cortisol and too many cytokines. This is my so-called amygdala hijack! Days after a traumatic event, my body remains caught in this amygdala hijack. The automatic reaction is when the prefrontal cortex—the part of the brain responsible for reason, decision-making, and problem-solving—is not working properly. The oxygen supply to the prefrontal cortex decreases because the body sends blood to the parts that need to fight or flee the danger.

When in survival mode, the body has no need for the prefrontal cortex. There isn't a need for any intellectual reasoning when you are facing a ferocious lion! You want to run as fast as you can. This is how our amazing bodies ensure our survival.

However, the scary part is that it is not the event that keeps the stress response active. It is my reaction to the story in my head that keeps activating the amygdala. My own thoughts are keeping me in amygdala-hijack mode. The more I stress, the more cortisol and cytokines I release into my body, causing constant inflammation and impairing my immune system. I make myself sick. The first thing I notice when stressed is a sore throat. The bout of shingles I had on my face is another perfect example of absolute physical agony caused by stress.

I am convinced all the illnesses were caused by the activation of this stress response, and of course, what I told myself after traumatic events. The story, running on a repeating loop in my head, is what contributed to my maladies.

*　　*　　*

I page back to the first event in my journal and see the fourteen-year-old girl sitting all alone on the pavilion again. What was the story I then told myself? *I am not good enough to fit in with this community.* This despite being the head girl in primary school, captain of the netball team, with many accolades and certificates for my academic achievements.

When I was rejected by the community and a circle of so-called friends, I was left with a feeling of total abandonment. I believed that there was something wrong with me, to be ostracized like that. Nobody cared about my inner deprivation and how I craved acceptance. *Nobody cares about a loser*, I told myself.

Our brains are wired for us to fit into a social system. It is another one of the survival tricks the brain plays. Our amygdalae are constantly scanning the environment for clues about whether we will fit in with the social system or not. If they detect a misfit, they sound the alarm.

"Poor child, I can see this girl was up against her own brain." It is that voice again.

"What do you mean, *this girl*? It is me! Are you back?" I must ask, because this is a bit unexpected.

"Don't go into drama mode, Rina. Stay in observer mode. Observe your life. Stay with me and observe. It is important," the voice almost begs. Then it continues: "Don't associate with the thoughts, the emotions, and the story. You are so much more than that. You are the soul, having lived the experience called *life*."

I am almost breathless as I try to make sense of the voice's instructions.

"Look at this life as if you are watching a movie," it continues. "There is a main character in the movie. When watching the movie, pay particular attention to the growth of the character.

You are the actress playing the role. You can safely watch the movie now. You are safe," the voice says with great empathy before concluding, "Do you know what a great privilege this is?"

I almost choke on my words. "Excuse me? *Privileged* to watch a movie of my own awful life story? I am almost fifty years old. Do you have any idea how much suffering I've accumulated over those years? I wasted so much precious time!"

"When you were in matric, we sent you an angel. She was one of your teachers at the time and was very fond of you. Now, remember when you tore ligaments in your feet playing netball at school? First the left foot, the next year the right?" the voice asks cautiously.

"Of course I remember. I was such a mess at the time. Always getting hurt in netball every year. It started when I was fourteen ..."

Here I stop myself.

"Yes, it started the day you told yourself you were not good enough. You always sabotaged your own success," the voice explains empathetically.

"I did that to myself? I hurt my back, broke my nose, tore my ligaments, all out of my own free will and own choice?" I am close to tears.

"It did not even stop there. You had depression, burnout, and after one of your business catastrophes, you contracted shingles and almost lost your hearing in the process. The one you probably want to talk about the least is the dystonia in your left foot," the voice drones on.

A wave of vicious anger starts welling up inside me. It is almost like a swell in the ocean, the water preparing to push a giant wave toward the shore, where it will crush and grind everything in its path.

"Your anger is not helpful," the voice observes. "As a matter of fact, it is just an emotion the actress feels in the movie. You are not the traumas, the pain, or the accompanying emotions. I want you to remain in observer mode. Now, remember the angel-teacher in your matric year?"

I am surprised that the voice has been with me for so long today. "OK, you make your point," I sigh. I still feel some anger and am a little confused now about who I should be, the observer or the participant.

"The teacher found you in the schoolyard, your foot bandaged. You were struggling to walk with crutches," the voice continues.

Really persistent to share something about the teacher, I half sarcastically think to myself. I remember that day like it was yesterday. I felt so sorry for myself, struggling like that. Life was sheer hell!

"Would you be able to recall what she said to you?" the voice asks. Then, before I can get a word in, the voice continues: "She said some people go through life born with the proverbial silver spoon in their mouths. They are ships on a calm sea, sailing with a perfect wind behind them. But when they arrive at the end of their lives, do they have any interesting stories to tell? Have they truly lived life? Other people sail rough seas, encounter enormous waves and storm winds, and survive tough times. They also get to the other side but have inspiring stories to tell. The teacher asked you a question that day at school. So now, you tell me: do you remember the question?"

As if I would forget. That moment is etched in my memory as if it happened yesterday. "She asked me what I want to do with my life, and I told her, *I want to sail the stormy seas with an inspiring story to tell!*" Recalling the interaction with the teacher, I can almost feel the young girl's excitement again, waiting to rush into life.

"Correct, and you gave her the right answer, considering your purpose," the voice adds.

"Why is that?" I ask, more curious now.

"How can you teach somebody to sail a ship on a stormy sea if you haven't done it before? What do you know about fearing for your life when a huge wave approaches the ship if you haven't experienced a similar wave yourself? Can you teach rejection, betrayal, depression, burnout, forgiveness, conditioning, surrender, control, and transcendence when you have no idea what it is? You will be asked: 'Have you walked this journey, conquered the lion, sailed the sea?' When you teach a concept, your students will ask if you have ever challenged your own beliefs. They will need reassurance that you could change your beliefs and that you have changed your brain from a state of turmoil to a state of peace." The passion with which the voice speaks is almost tangible. A silence descends between us.

The silence emphasizes the following words that echo through my head: *Have you wrestled with an angel*? The silence falls like a thick woolen blanket, and then the voice speaks again.

"Have you wrestled with an angel, like Jacob in his sleep?"

The silence reverberates through me. And then the voice booms, "You can only teach what you have learned."

A well-known quote by Richard Bach suddenly comes to me: "You teach best what you most need to learn."

CHAPTER 13

A Series of Patterns

Outside, dusk is falling. I stare at the words on the laptop in front of me. What am I missing? There must be a pattern here, but where? I keep coming back to the same paragraph on the screen. There must be a message there. Slowly, I reread it again.

> *The words cut through my body like a cold, sharp knife. The blade slices through me in slow motion. It starts as acute pain in my head, disorienting me. The sensation moves down to contract my throat. It grips my heart with ice and sucks the air from my lungs. Nausea rises in my stomach, and my legs start to tremble. I am paralyzed and cold, feeling cut off from the life source. Then very slowly, I feel life creeping back, warm blood flowing, and heat returning to my body. Is this what shock feels like?*
>
> *I go through the next few days like an automatic robot.*

Leaning back in my chair, still looking at the words on the screen, I open my mind and broaden my awareness to take in the whole room. It is a technique I have learned in psychology, called *peripheral focus*.

I normally use this in facilitation to ensure I stay aware of all in the audience while focusing on an individual delegate.

Peripheral vision enables one to see objects in a 180-degree view. This helps me keep an awareness of everything in front of me without moving my head.

At this specific moment, the paragraph on the screen is in front of me, but to my right, my stacked bookshelf is in vision too. The words on the screen and a book on the shelf seem to blend. The words that jump out at me are *head, throat, lungs, heart, stomach, legs.* At the same time, the green book on the shelf swims clearly toward me. I lean forward in my office chair to grab it, almost tipping myself over in the process, but I manage to hold on and safely land back on the wheels with a loud clunk. All the while, my eyes are glued to the screen—hypnotized by the words. Only now do I read the title of the book: *Eastern Body, Western Mind* by Anodea Judith.

I only scan the first few pages, as I have read the book several times before. Then, slowly, I read the following: "The chakra system is a seven-leveled philosophical model. A chakra is a center of organization that receives, assimilates, and expresses life force energy."

This means there is energy all around us, I think to myself.

The best example of an energy force I have observed is a tree. Ten years ago, we built a wooden deck at our holiday home. On the right corner was a small thorn tree, its trunk only about six centimeters in diameter at the time. We fenced the deck with wooden poles, ending with two poles pointing at the tree, with gaps of thirty centimeters on each side.

Two years later, sitting on the deck with a sundowner in my hand, I noticed a strange phenomenon. The thorn tree had grown; its trunk was much thicker. However, where the wooden poles were pointing at the trunk, it was obviously thinner, even though the poles were in no way touching or obstructing growth. I realized that the tree must have an energy field around it. Though the tree itself was far away from the fence, its energy field was probably touching it, and in this way, tree and fence accommodated each other.

As the years went by, the phenomenon continued. At some stage, the tree apparently decided it was strong enough and started to grow back into the space at the fence. There were no longer any obvious gaps. I have always wondered what dynamics I had observed but believe that it had to do with the energy fields of the tree and the fence.

Since then, I have read many books explaining the energy fields of people and objects. Therefore, I am most comfortable with the idea of the existence of energy wheels within us. These wheels receive, assimilate, and even distribute energy to all our body parts.

Wholly engrossed in Judith's book, I lean back in my chair to reflect on her ideas. Suddenly, it all becomes clear to me.

There seem to be two forces at work. One force wants to express itself in physical matter. Could this be our souls wishing to have a physical experience? The idea to express starts as a thought in the head and then finds its way toward physical expression? That could be the head-to-toe experience. Life energy enters the brain and finds its expression by creating a physical experience.

The other force works the opposite way. There is a soul that knows we are part of a universal expression, and it is longing to go back to the Source from which it received its idea. The body knows we are light beings.

I read, "The seven vortices of the chakras are created by the combination of these two active principles: consciousness and matter. We can think of the flow of consciousness as entering through the crown chakra and moving down through the body. Since the chakras represent elements that become increasingly dense as they descend."

It would seem then that every time I had gone through a trauma and the subsequent shock response, I influenced the turning of my energy wheels. It is almost as if I switched off or dimmed my own energy efficiency in these instances. Like at night, when you switch off or dim the lights when going to bed. The specific paragraph on the computer screen seems to zoom larger, and I read it out to myself again.

> *The words cut through my body like a cold, sharp knife. The blade slices through me in slow motion. It starts as acute pain in my head, disorienting me. The sensation moves down to contract my throat. It grips my heart with ice and sucks the air from my lungs. Nausea rises in my stomach, and my legs start to tremble. I am paralyzed and cold,* **feeling cut off from the life source.** *Then very slowly, I feel life creeping back, warm blood flowing, and heat returning to my body. Is this what shock feels like?*
>
> *I go through the next few days like an automatic robot.*

I highlight *"cut off from the life source."* Every time we react with this type of stress response to an experience in life, we cut ourselves off from the life source and jeopardize our own energy bodies. Because of this, illness can manifest.

Having worked in the corporate world, I imagine an energy field much the same as the culture in an organization. This culture is not necessarily visible, but the employees in that organization will tell you, "This is the way we behave around here."

I find the energy field very similar. It is the culture in which the body's cells must do their work, and we cannot measure or see it. It is just how the cells behave because "this is the way we behave around here."

In an organization, the top executives or thinkers set the culture. In the body, that function would be performed by the brain, our thinking system. It is the culture that sets the tone in which our body's cells will function. And everybody knows what a catastrophic impact a toxic culture can have on an organization.

The same is probably true for my body. I now realize what the impact of my thinking system was on my body. It is neatly summarized in "*I go through the next few days like an automatic robot.*"

My awareness of "self" and everything around me was significantly impaired on these occasions. It is shocking what suffering we can inflict on ourselves through our toxic thought processes.

By analyzing my stress patterns, I learn that the seven energy wheels function as energy sources to all the organs in my body. The energy is then provided to the different layers of my physiology. This energetic structure supports life, where it feeds every cell, organ, and system in my body. When dimming or impairing this energy flow, I deprive my own body of its critical life energy.

This shows that one can read many books and have an intellectual understanding of the content, but only when noticing how things play out in practice do we become aware of what we are doing to our bodies.

A wisdom model I always draw for my colleagues suddenly springs to mind. I grab a piece of blank paper and start drawing the model the way I would usually explain it to my colleagues. However, this time I am explaining it to myself.

It starts with a diagonal line from the bottom left, going up to the right. This line is titled *knowledge*. When we attend a course or read a book, we grasp the theory intellectually. This is the way we grow our knowledge base. I have read many books about energy and the energy system, which is the theory.

However, there is more. Next, I draw another diagonal line from the bottom right, going up to the left, crossing the *knowledge* line midway. The second line is called *experience*.

In my life of fifty years, I have gained a great deal of experience in these energy centers. Every shock, trauma, or challenge in my life can be connected to a physical illness. The dystonia in my foot manifested from my roots and the feelings of rejection or not being good enough. It is probably also a sign that I struggle to find my own movement or flow. Many teachers and instructors have, over time, advised me to let go and let things flow.

My stomach issues were severe around the time when my business relationships failed and I started questioning my own identity.

High blood pressure was diagnosed when I had to deal with loss and forgiveness. The shingles affected my tongue when I struggled to express my true identity, and felt I had to dim my light. I can link an illness with every energy center in my body, and I can vouch for a condition on every level or center.

Looking at the line drawing again, I circle the point where the knowledge and experience lines cross. X marks the spot where I have gained boundless knowledge and experience. This is the point where you become the expert. It is only when looking at the trauma-emotion-illness pattern of my own life that I realize the direct relationship between experiences I had gone through and the ailments I had suffered. This *aha* is where my knowledge of and experience with the chakra system suddenly come together at the *expert* point.

Everything is indeed energy. When my negative emotions blocked the energy flow to specific areas of my body, an illness would strike somewhere in that area. The story playing in my head made me ill.

This is possibly the reason experts in the field refer to it as *dis-ease* rather than *disease*. It makes so much more sense. My toxic emotions caused discomfort in a specific area, which then caused a toxic culture for the body cells, which in turn became dis-eased.

But my model is still incomplete. From the *expert* point, I draw a line straight down, ending off with a circle. It looks as if the circle is dangling between the words *knowledge* and *experience*. In the circle, I write *wisdom*.

"This is the point where *knowledge, experience,* and *expertise* are transcended," the teacher in me says out loud. "It is only then that *wisdom* emerges." I end my self-teaching dramatically, stabbing at the word with my favorite turquoise pen.

Looking at my theory and diagram, I feel very proud of my discovery, but apparently this is a rather one-sided feeling.

"You are not there yet," the voice whispers softly, and before I can express any surprise at its presence, it adds more forcefully, *"Heal the sick."*

And then there is silence.

I know the voice is gone.

CHAPTER 14

A Clay Tablet

"If you could write ten brain powers on clay tablets to send into the world, what would you include?" I ask my online audience, most of them psychologists. I want to test their neuroscience knowledge and see if they genuinely understand what they can do to empower their clients. The brain is a mighty organ, and so often, we underestimate its true powers.

"You have ten minutes to write down your answers," I conclude and mute my computer to allow them time to put their thinking caps on.

"If you could write seven life lessons on a clay tablet, what would they be?" The voice is playful, imitating me.

"Oh no, not you again!" I whisper. "I am in a training session. Go away!" I did not know that you could whisper in your head, but I think that is what I just did.

"I know you are training. It is the only time you spontaneously listen without analyzing too much," the voice continues playfully.

"What do you mean?" I whisper again.

"Haven't you noticed?" the voice continues. "You are very wise and knowledgeable when you train, coach, or read books. Haven't you observed that you know things about others and your audience without them telling you anything? Don't you think there is help coming from somewhere? You are such a difficult person to convince because your logical, realistic, scientific brain always stands in the way. You believe that what you see is what there is. But there is much, much more that you are not even aware of."

"Oh, please," I whisper, rolling my eyes. *I really hope this is not a "you should be grateful for all the help you get from us" sermon,* I think silently to myself.

"Well, then, teach me all there is to see," I challenge the voice, sounding braver than I feel. The voice does not bother to respond to my dare.

Ten minutes have ticked by, and I need to get back to the online audience. I quickly jot down on my notepad, *If you could write seven life lessons on a clay tablet, what would they be?*

I roll my eyes again, a bit irritated. The voice was being helpful, but its timing was a bit off!

The audience members start their feedback, and I am pleased with their inputs and insight. It is an excellent session, and the interaction and learning process have worked to everybody's benefit. We end the session on a high note. I can't leave the screen session quickly enough, though, and I grab my notepad to start working on my life lesson list.

*   *   *

Instead of contemplating my seven life lessons, as the voice suggested, and running the risk of getting stuck again, I decide on something else. I want to see if I can divide some principles of the brain into the seven energy centers. It sounds like fun to me, and considering the session we just had, the brain theory is still recent, so this should be an easy and exciting exercise.

I draw two columns on the notepad. Heading the first, I write *Energy Centers*. The second column is headed *Brain Systems*. As I have noticed in books, I decide to start with the energy centers from the bottom up. The first center is assigned its familiar name: *survival or root center*. In the brain column, I add: *The brain is programmed for automatic survival and avoidance of pain*. The brain assists the body to avoid getting hurt or experiencing physical pain. The whole limbic system is designed to fulfill this role.

I ponder this fact for a moment. There definitely is a mechanism in the brain that supports the first energy center and ensures our safety. The limbic system prefers safety and security, the behavior we need for survival.

The same procedure is repeated with the second center. I know center two has something to do with feelings and emotion. So, what does the brain do about feelings? Oh yes, the brain is wired to read and respond to emotion. The limbic system is again playing a role here. It helps us to easily fit into social situations when we notice the behavior and emotions of others. We also apply emotional strategies to avoid emotional pain and seek pleasure. I can tick-off center two.

The third center is the powerhouse. It is usually referred to as the *solar plexus*. This center relies heavily on our self-esteem, our unique identity, and our sense of personal power. However, it is a positive power, like the feeling of empowerment. What is in the brain that supports this center? This is easy to explain: The brain is goal-seeking by nature. When we set goals, the reticular activating system, referred to as RAS, will let information through that supports our stated goals.

The RAS is a network of interconnected neurons in the brain stem. It assists our ability to pay attention. We continuously receive millions of tiny bits of information that flow through the brain. This is the network that filters the information and only brings that which is important to our attention. The brain supports the idea of empowerment twice, as we also have the *nucleus accumbens*, which plays a role in the brain's reward circuit.

When we reach our goals and the brain recognizes the achievement, it releases dopamine, a neurotransmitter. Dopamine is a chemical messenger that makes us feel good, provides energy, and helps us chase our goals. Our systems are wired to use our power, exercise our will, reach our goals, live our unique selves, and be successful.

I sit back in my chair, barely noticing the birds frolicking in the birdbath outside the window of my study at home and not wanting to lose my focus on my seven-centers exercise.

Totally intrigued by the way the table is developing, I cannot wait to continue adding details to the columns. Although I have been studying the brain for years now, the possibility has never occurred to me that my brain can support the energy centers.

Thinking about my wisdom model, I realize that some wisdom is only filtering through to me now. So much for my expertise on brain theory!

I now realize that everything is indeed interconnected. Every theory has a piece of universal truth. The Eastern and Western theories are just not connected yet. However, it is our responsibility to wake up and search for these truths. We have the power to make these connections and complete the picture.

I can't wait to uncover the next pearl of wisdom. Center four is the heart center. The brain is wired for connections and relationships. The cingulate gyrus and the insula in the brain trigger the secretion of oxytocin, a hormone associated with empathy, social connection, and trust.

Oxytocin is often described as the love hormone. It is also known for its role during the bonding process between a mother and her child. Yes, the brain supports connection and love!

Center five relates to our voice and communication. The brain uses language as a major tool to activate and manipulate the environment, and the environment is wired to support this. I have read somewhere that not only do our cells respond to voice and language, but atoms do too. The book *The Hidden Messages in Water* by Masaru Emoto explores this phenomenon well.

To me, the wonder lies not only in the fact that water responds to language but the other way around. We are wired to communicate with our environment, and in return, our environment is wired to understand this communication. Does that mean we are wired to influence matter and cocreate our own reality in this world? It seems we have the machinery to do it. So, there could be some truth in it.

I heave a deep sigh. I am so proud of myself for how I have managed this exercise so far. Center six is also an easy one. Here I write: *The brain is wired to set intent and visions.* The brain performs creative cognitive functions, such as projecting and building models of the future The prefrontal cortex plays a role in this ability. It can manipulate and transform current models to see the world through new mental pictures.

We are wired to see visions, as well as the part we are to play in these bigger visions. We can see beyond the obvious and imagine the future. Then we can start creating these visions in reality by using our voice from center five and our will from center three. Furthermore, we can convince others to support us by using our social connection capability from center four. The brain is indeed a powerful machine!

I write *center seven* on the page. How is the brain wired for spirituality? Is it at all wired for a spiritual experience? And then it hits me. A book by Rick Strassman, *DMT: The Spirit Molecule*, springs to mind, and I pull it from my bookshelf to page through again. And bang! There it is: the brain is structured to produce and fancy a spirit molecule. A lot of research is still needed in this area, but it is something to explore. I will keep my eyes and ears open for more developments in this field in the future.

I put my pen down, very proud of myself. But then my eyes find their way back to the initial question on the notepad: *If you could write seven life lessons on a clay tablet, what would they be?*

Suppose all the thoughts we ever thought and all the knowledge we ever gathered were stored in books in an extensive library in our subconscious. In that case, I can imagine a tiny Rina now vigorously paging through all the books to find the answer. She is running from shelf to shelf to find something even vaguely applicable to answer this question.

*   *   *

I do not find the answer I am looking for in this round. However, I do find a memory from long ago. I was in my early twenties, going to interview for a position as organizational development and training manager at a large corporation. At the interview, I had to complete a psychometric test conducted by a psychologist who later became my manager and mentor. Yes, the interview was a success, and I still regard this person as the best leader and mentor I ever had the pleasure to work for. This was the same perfect leader I had at a later stage to tell I was resigning from my perfect job and perfect salary in search of a not-so-perfect purpose.

The assessment took the format of an interview. Even today, I can recall it almost word for word.

"What is your dream for the future?" Andrew asked.

"I want to write a theory similar to that of a Freud or a Jung. This theory will help people to understand," I glibly answered.

"Understand what?" Andrew tried to get more information on my somewhat random statement.

"I have no idea. I don't even know where that answer came from," I replied, totally surprising myself.

I can still recall how baffled I was by my own answer. However, now that I am older and hopefully wiser, that incident makes more sense. I always tell delegates attending my training sessions that the subconscious never lies. The subconscious mind knows so many things. The answers always hover around somewhere inside us. We *do* know the answers, and we just need to remember what we know.

I look at the question on the notepad again: *If you could write seven life lessons on a clay tablet, what would they be?* I smile. I know I am close to the answer to this question. It is just a matter of time.

Time has slipped away quietly while I was trying to unravel the secrets of the subconscious. When I look up, it is already dark outside. *What a wonderfully productive day*, I think, stiffly getting up from behind my desk.

Tired but invigorated, I switch off the light in the study on my way out. At that moment, my brain makes another connection: "Write down the revelation and make it plain on tablets"— Habakkuk 2:2.

CHAPTER 15

The Miracles

It is the end of 2019, and I have finally concluded that my life's primary purpose is *healing through teaching*.

I also finally can confirm that my major calling or mission is to write a book with all my experiences and teachings, plus pearls of wisdom gathered from others. All these together form my life lessons. People will heal through reading my story, something I find most comforting. Having experienced the Universe by now, I know those who don't need it will not buy the book anyway.

But I still need to write the conclusion. I even have an idea that I might be missing a chapter or two. My publisher has phoned a few times to check on my progress, and every time my answer is the same: *I am nearly there*. I am done with the years of experimenting and observation. This is an excellent year to finally publish my book.

I am looking forward to celebrating my fiftieth birthday. My health has improved substantially, and the consulting business is thriving. Looking back, it has been a fantastic year and my best year in business ever!

Then COVID-19 hits the world at full force. There are no warning signs, and nothing has prepared us for the onslaught of a virus that will change the world overnight.

Countries the world over, South Africa included, announce strict lockdown regulations to cope with the pandemic. I wait for my body's shock reaction, but nothing happens. It seems I have that under control this time.

All businesses start to work from home. To keep my team creative and focused, I decide to take our consulting business online. We focus our energy on producing videos and releasing online training material. These new creative processes are incredibly stimulating and bring a fun element to our work.

The moment I catch myself having a negative thought, I immediately block it and repeat over and over to myself: *I will trust the process, and I will trust the river of flow.*

Sitting in my study at home, now my day-to-day office, I am working on a training presentation. All is quiet, and I am in deep concentration making last-minute changes to the document.

"What can I teach you?" the voice asks.

"You! Where were you all this time? What do you mean, *what can you teach me*?" I ask, confused.

"You asked me before to teach you. Remember?" the voice asks.

"I do, but that was just a dare, ages ago. Now you want to take up my dare in the middle of a worldwide lockdown! What the heck?" I reply in total surprise.

However, I immediately start wondering what it is I want to learn. I know my previous answer would have been, *Teach me about finances, teach me about money, teach me how to get more clients, teach me to build up this huge consulting firm that I always dreamt of.* But here we are in the middle of a lockdown, and suddenly, none of these things matter anymore.

"Teach me about miracles," I hear myself saying with excitement.

What! Did I just say that?

"Teach me to see small miracles," I hear myself repeat.

Rina, are you out of your mind? You get one wish from the genie, and you ask to see small miracles every day? What on earth is wrong with you? It is in the middle of the COVID-19 pandemic, and you ask for miracles!

"I'll teach you to see," says the voice, and then there is silence. I know the voice is gone.

Not a voice for a lot of words or any small talk. That's for sure.

*   *   *

Early the following day, a gift arrives in my inbox. It is an autobiography by Lorna Byrne, *Angels in My Hair.* She writes about her communication with spiritual beings like angels, souls, and God. Rather an interesting choice of gift. I am a very rational, logic-minded person—more of a scientist than a mystic. However, I download and start reading the book. This is the one thing I have learned over the years: trust the Universe's choice of books.

The brain is a fascinating organ. Once you hold a belief, mainly in the subconscious mind, the brain will send information to support that belief. I look at my notepad, where I have jotted down this principle. It links with my insights on the energy centers and the brain. The reticular activation system (RAS), a network of neurons located in the brain stem, sends information of importance to us, particularly where our senses are concerned.

Normally, different types of information are forwarded by the brain and the RAS. These would include information needed for survival, about goals or intent, and of course, supporting beliefs. And this is precisely what starts to play out for me. The more I read Lorna Byrne's book, the more I become aware of the miracles around me.

Our beautiful garden is a luscious haven of green, as if to compensate for the sadness currently in the world. I also notice a variety of birds chirping and whistling in the trees and bushes outside, many of which I have not seen before. Lorna says that birds are messengers from angels.

I finally launch my first talk on our company's YouTube channel. Even that is a miracle to me! When some of the technology plays up, I catch myself asking an angel for help. And, lo and behold, everything works perfectly!

Simple miracles are happening daily. I suddenly find things lost some time ago. People who left in the past return to me. Friends phone from overseas to tell me how much they care for me. Former mentees call to say how much they learned from me and how my teachings have impacted their lives.

I find beauty in the colors of flowers and the feathers of birds. I start to see the world from a different angle. Suddenly, I see it through the lens of small miracles. Something in my "seeing" shifts.

*   *   *

The way I start to see differently reminds me of a discussion with my mentor many years ago. I was busy with my doctoral thesis at the time, overwhelmed by the amount of information I had to make sense of. One day, he explained to me that the process of discovering new theories could be compared to swimming in a pool of natural water.

At first, you are at the bottom of the pool, stuck in the thick mud of information. You are trying to find a spot you can push yourself up from, and you intend to swim up to clearer water. Then you find that specific point in the mud and push.

Next, you are floating in the water just above the mud. The water is still clouded with grass and pieces of mud. You search through all the information around you and can then swim up a little higher. The water is getting clearer, and you think you can make sense of what you see around you. For the first time, you can see farther, and you can identify objects some distance away.

Again, you sift through information, now almost swimming just under the surface of the water. The water becomes crystal clear, and you can make sense of everything that is below you in the pool. Now you can "see" the usefulness of the mud in relation to where you are. Suddenly it makes sense. The mud served its purpose by offering you a stable point from which to push yourself up.

At this point, you can see the surface of the water just above you. There is clarity of the other objects around you. You will also note that being just under the water's surface, you can look at the world outside the water as well.

My mentor emphasized that new theory and new philosophy are only discovered by the strong and the brave who break through the surface of the water. Imagine that moment when you watch somebody swimming underwater, and suddenly they break through the surface. What a sight! My mentor is of the opinion that most people are so content with what they see just under the surface of the water that they never put in that last effort to break through.

He told this story to encourage me to delve deeper for those meta insights of my study, something most students would not do. Searching for meta insights was a new skill I would put to good use later in life too.

The picture of the pool of water, muddy below and clear just under the surface, has always stayed in my mind. During my own life journey, I would ask myself the question: *Where am I in this process? Have I broken the surface to arrive at meta insights yet?*

*   *   *

Lorna Byrne's books *Angels in My Hair* and *Angels at My Fingertips* come to me at a time when I most needed them. Suddenly able to appreciate small miracles, I feel as though life is starting to make more sense. I start noticing the world outside, above the surface of the water. Patterns and shapes are beginning to make sense to me.

As is my routine these days, I wake up early. Slumped against the kitchen counter, I watch the orange light of morning illuminate the room while waiting for the coffee machine to work its magic. Still half-soothed by sleep, I sink into a deep reverie.

What is the difference between the concepts *interwoven* and *interlinked*? The hardships I encountered in my business life come back to me, one by one. Each of these visions is accompanied by the faces of the people who were part of it all. The faces of two business partners in particular appear in my mind's eye, and I feel a pain shoot through my heart.

"Have you really forgiven them?" the voice asks.

"Of course I have," I reply rather unconvincingly.

"Then why are you still lashing out at them?" the voice responds.

"OK, I get it. I forgive them with my whole heart," I reply.

I wait, but there is dead silence.

"And in your soul?" the voice asks.

"I forgive them with my soul," I say.

An indescribable peace fills me.

I think the voice has left, but I ask the question anyway: "While you are here, can you please answer a question for me? Why on earth did all these people have to go through this pain? Why did they meet me? Why was it necessary in the first place?" I hold my breath, not sure if there will be an answer.

"Have you noticed that you often quote to others a line from the book *In Pursuit of Purpose* by Miles Munroe: 'Your life contains something that this generation needs?' Do you understand what you quote to others? Do you understand the implication that *your life contains something that this generation needs*? the voice asks.

"I think I am beginning to understand," I whisper, too scared to move in case I lose this moment of truth. My breath comes in shallow puffs as I anxiously anticipate a response from the voice.

Suddenly, there is a crystal-clear vision. The face of every person I have ever had a conflict with appears before me. At the same time, I hear the voice say, "Their lives contained something that *you* needed. If not for them, your book would not exist. You would not have a story to tell. So, did your life hold something they needed? Yes, they needed *you* there also to be able to tell their own stories."

"They needed me to hurt them?" I ask in a small voice.

"No, they needed *something*. Something you did, something you said. Something about you. You will never know what, but trust that they needed it!" says the voice.

"But I feel so sorry for them and ..."

The voice interrupts me mid-sentence and suddenly becomes quite authoritative. "That is the end of it! We will not talk about this again. You were needed, and they were needed. It is over."

I know it is not only the end of this conversation. It is the end of this connection for the morning.

The coffee machine pips up, and I smell the aroma of freshly brewed morning coffee. In slow motion, still half-frozen in the vision I have just had, I take two mugs from the cupboard.

So, that's it. It is that simple. This is what it means to be interconnected. People are playing specific roles for one another. We need each other to learn our life lessons and grow.

I say a silent prayer. I pray that every person who ever touched my life will know that I needed them. When they reflect on their lives, I pray that they will also find the things they needed out of my life from those interactions with me. I pray that they will be free.

I really need that coffee now. It is a typical bright and crisp winter morning in the middle of the COVID-19 pandemic lockdown in South Africa. Even the birds are still asleep in their nests. This time of the morning, they usually jump from tree to tree, branch to lawn, searching for their breakfast. Today, nothing is moving outside yet.

I pour two mugs of coffee, put them on a tray, and look at the garden through my kitchen window.

I start smiling.

"We should talk more in the mornings. I learn a lot when we talk," I tease.

Dead silence.

"I know you're there," I add, trying harder to get a reaction.

Still looking at the winter garden, I notice a few birds, coming from nowhere, starting to hop around in the big tree just outside the window. "I know what you're doing. You want to distract my attention with the birds," I say, trying to connect with the voice again.

As I pick up the tray to take our coffee to the bedroom, a one-liner scampers through my head, almost like somebody walking away from me, teasingly calling over his shoulder, "Oh, and by the way … the Universe is mischievous!"

CHAPTER 16

The Ladder

Now that the book is complete, I need a title. I have played around with different ideas over the years but cannot pick one yet. It feels as if I am missing the final piece of my jigsaw puzzle.

I worked hard putting the final touches to the book today, and it is already quite late when I finally put my laptop away. Exhausted, I get into bed and fall asleep almost immediately.

I wake up in the middle of the night. My cell phone is ringing on my bedside table. It is my publisher, calling from the United States.

This is weird. They know I am in South Africa and that there is a big difference in our time zones. I have never had such a late call from them before. We have a short conversation, as the caller just wants to check how my writing is progressing. I give my usual assurance that all is well. Disconnecting the call, I fall back on my pillow.

"That's it? You call in the middle of the night just for that?" I ask nobody in particular, still a bit disorientated by the late-night call. Snuggling down, I pull the duvet back up around my shoulders.

At this stage, I am in a deep alpha brain state, still on my way to theta, the sleeping state. Alpha is that state of the brain where the conscious and the subconscious merge. In hypnosis, this is the state psychologists regard as the golden opportunity to suggest something they want the person to remember forever.

"Title the book *The Ladder of Jacob*," the voice says.

"Why?" I ask but immediately fall into deep theta sleep.

*   *   *

The next morning, I wake up and straight away remember the last instruction from the voice. I have a title for my book. It was given to me at precisely the right time: asleep enough to make a lasting impression and awake enough to remember it the following day.

It is still not quite light outside when I open my laptop to find out more about Jacob's dream. I remember the story from the Bible, but the details are a bit hazy. I find myself googling almost every book or piece of information that mentions something about Jacob and his dream about the ladder.

Of course, the best place to read and learn about Jacob is in the Bible, Genesis 28:12 (NLT). I start reading his dream over and over.

> As he slept, he dreamed of a stairway that reached from the earth up to heaven. And he saw the angels of God going up and down the stairway. Then Jacob awoke from his sleep and said, "Surely the Lord is in this place, and I wasn't even aware of it!" But he was also afraid and said, "What an awesome place this is! It is none other than the house of God, the very gateway to heaven!"

For the next three days, I read and research nonstop. But I still don't understand why this title the voice gave me in the middle of the night is so significant. I ask the Universe for help.

My hammer, as for Thor, arrives on my Kindle in the form of *Edward Cayce's Amazing Interpretation of the Revelation* by John van Auken.

Sitting outside on the porch enjoying nature, I continue my research by reading this new book. And what a revelation! I have been a bad student of the Universe up to now. I suddenly realize things are there right in front of my eyes, and I keep missing them. This discovery is as much of a shock to me as it must have been to Jacob at the time.

The reference in Jacob's dream to "this place" is nothing other than my own being. It is my own consciousness. It is the dwelling place of God. It is the house or temple of God.

"The Lord is in this place." When I am silent and I go inside, I will find Him there. He is within this silent place. He is always dwelling in this place. He is waiting for us to meet Him there.

"The stairway leads to the gateway to heaven." I climb this ladder of consciousness every day of my life. Every life lesson aims at teaching me to move my consciousness up the ladder. It wants me to understand the ultimate peace and the ultimate love. Angels are there to meet me and help me up the ladder. There is an angel for every energy center, and therefore, for every consciousness level or plane.

This is, then, my last life lesson. This is the lesson where everything comes together at last. It is the final rung of my own ladder, and it is all about understanding the last plane. The ladder is my gift: the moment when it all finally comes together.

* * *

Suddenly, my purpose makes sense. "Go and announce to them that the Kingdom of Heaven is near. Heal the sick." I now realize that the kingdom of heaven is within every person. Although I embrace the idea of meeting God within, my experience with the

Divine has always been a feeling of outsideness, which is due to my own projection.

When light passes through a projector, it casts an enlarged picture on a screen. Similarly, light is in me, but the projected experience takes place outside me. All external experiences I have are therefore flowing from my internal processes and projection. It is as if my body is the projector.

The way I filter the descending force or light is the way my external environment manifests. My internal processes or planes of consciousness directly impact what happens in my environment—my screen, so to speak. The story I project is the story that manifests in my outside environment. The conclusion is that I project my stories from different consciousness planes. Furthermore, it is possible to ascend or descend between these planes.

At the time when I was living my life experiences, I always had a strong feeling that these were happening externally. Any indication or signal that something was occurring inside me was so weak that I missed it. I also did not apply any insight I might have gained from previous events or stories. In the process, I failed to rise to a better understanding of awareness of such experiences. I was also oblivious to the fact that I was the cause of many of these experiences.

Every day, I create my own life—a life based mainly on my own lifelong thought patterns created by repeated traumas. Sadly, this was not a story reflecting my true potential. The mere act of looking with the expectation that something does exist may precisely be the force that creates it into existence.

It reminds me of what Neville Goddard said: "Man's chief delusion is his conviction that there are causes other than his own state of consciousness."

Neville Goddard and Edgar Cayce refer to the life principle that we must have an *ideal* to strive for. At first, I did not understand what they meant, but it is making sense to me now. Both explain that there is a huge difference between mental and spiritual processing. My understanding is then that we must hold a spiritual *ideal* or intent.

Through mental processing, the mind will create a clear picture or blueprint to manifest this intent. While with our bodies, we will engage in physical activities to create this picture. Without this clear intent and blueprint picture for our lives, we will build random realities and fall victim to circumstances. I feel slightly better to also read that this is a life principle that most people misunderstand.

* * *

I continue reading the work of Goddard. "You know a thing mentally by looking at it from the outside, by comparing it and defining it. By thinking of it. Whereas you can know a thing spiritually only by becoming it, only by thinking from it. You must be the thing itself and not merely talk about it or look at it."

I look up just in time to see a bird soar high over my house. It flaps farther and farther away, becoming just a tiny black speck and then merging and becoming blue sky. *Exactly like that*, I think.

Hold an ideal. My soul holds the ideal. My mind forms thoughts, thereby building the ideal. My physical world then becomes that ideal because I am physically creating it.

The big secret is to hold on to that ideal with discipline, attention, and complete focus. A wise person once said, "Live with intention, attention, and no tension."

All ideals already exists as mere possibilities, I learned from quantum physics. I can access the ideal by thinking about it and building it with my thoughts. But I can also think *from* it—act as if it already exists. This is how I can transform myself into the ideal image.

Herbert Puryear, an author, also interpreting Cayce's work, said, "It is only when we take charge of our own thoughts and give them positive direction, that we achieve a major step in our soul development."

I look up again. I see another bird fly over my house, then farther away, becoming a speck and eventually also becoming one with the blue sky.

Still staring at where the bird has disappeared, I wonder: *How ambitious can we be with this ideal?*

I continue reading Puryear: "God created man in His image; more specifically it is the soul that is created in the image of God. Thus, the soul possesses all the attributes and aspects of the nature of the Divine. To say that we are made in His image indicates that no matter how far astray we may go, there still remains within us the pattern of and the link to perfection through which we may regain full attunement with the Whole."

Again I look up into the sky, letting the words sink into my soul. Another bird flies overhead, farther and farther away, disappearing at almost the exact spot where the other two birds had. What is it with the birds today? Then I remember Lorna Byrne's idea that birds are messengers from angels.

Looking down at Puryear's book still in my hands, my eyes catch the following phrase: "Ye are gods; and all of you are children of the Most High." I can't remember that I have read this in the Bible before, so I page around and then find Psalm 82:6 (NLT) and read, "You are gods; you are all children of the Most High."

It is right here! Right in front of my eyes. The further explanation makes sense: we are all created as perfect spiritual beings out of God's desire for companionship, to be cocreators with Him. It makes sense then that we can use this akashic field—the presence of an interconnecting cosmic field at the roots of reality—to form and manifest this ideal. We are *from* this, and we *are* this, and we can *create* this. Then it makes sense why the environment reacts to our voice.

I pick up Gregg Braden and read:

> If the particles we are made of can be in instantaneous communication with one another, exist in two places at once, live in the past and the present, then we can, too. The only difference between those isolated particles and us is that we're made of a lot of them held together by the power of consciousness itself. The single most powerful force in the universe lives within each of us. And that is the great secret of creation itself: the power to create in the world what we imagine in our beliefs.

Somewhere in the depth of our soul's memory, we remember that we have miracle powers, we can create miracles, and we are the miracle itself.

I look up again, just to see another bird fly over the house, farther and farther away, till it becomes a speckle and then disappears in the blue sky. And then I suddenly remember the modern word for *akasha*: sky!

"I know what you are doing. I have noticed," I say softly.

And then more to myself, as an afterthought: "You are still a bit slow at this. It took four birds! The Universe demonstrated the principle to you, and it took four birds for you to notice! The Universe is indeed mischievous!"

Chapter 17

A Moment in the Theatre, Part One

It is still early morning. An amber glow is just starting to show on the horizon, and birds are welcoming a new day with song and sound. "Oh, my favorite time of day," I mumble, still floating in that space between asleep and awake.

I must have fallen back to sleep again, because I dream of being in a theatre called Akasha. In a hall to the side of the theater, posters of countless movie titles are displayed. I look at all the many different titles in wonder and then slowly walk through to the theater itself.

"I love movies that combine science and the mystic," I say to myself. "I must have changed. Previously, I would have preferred just science. Now I want to watch something that will appeal to the logic part of my brain but also connect to the intuitive."

Inside the theater, I find a seat and wait for a movie that is about to start. There is a flicker on the screen, and the first scene opens. However, strangely enough, the movie does not begin with a story. It starts with the film crew and actors still in a planning session, exploring the set, theme, and different characters.

In this backstage scene, the crew decides a life story of an entrepreneur will play out against the development of a consulting business. They debate how the main character will search for her mission on earth, which she will discover at some point during her life.

The twist in the story is that the main character is both observer and participant in her life story. There will be a series of tests, like life experiments. These tests will create growth in awareness or consciousness in the character.

After a thorough explanation, all the participants nod in agreement. They agree to play their part in the story. They all understand the story and their roles in it.

An interesting aspect of the movie is that there is no predetermined script. It will be an artificial intelligence script, which means the script evolves with the story. Nobody knows how the story will unfold, as it will depend on the choices of the main character. Again, the participants nod in agreement. They will make it up as the story unfolds. The planning scene stops.

* * *

There is a moment of darkness in the theatre. I sink deeper in my seat to make myself more comfortable to watch the movie. I relax my shoulders and give a deep sigh. Music fills the theater from huge speakers, and then the first images fill the screen. The story has started.

I watch the character being born and how she lives out her youth. Even at an early age, she shows signs of a curious and sharp mind, but at the same time, her heart is sensitive, fragile, caring, and filled with a love for beauty. There is a subtle hint that there will be a serious conflict between her heart and her mind throughout her life. One cannot help but wonder which will win, the brain or the heart?

Every movie has a hero, and every hero has a mission and must unravel the magical way that mission will succeed. The same is true for the main character in this story. Part of the plot is that it takes years before she unravels *the way*. In short, *the way* is all about a ladder. It is about ascending and descending the ladder of life.

Two major energetic forces are driving the character's progress on the ladder. The one force is top-down, descending, and the other is bottom-up, ascending. The descending force is a powerful urge to manifest the spiritual instruction of healing in a concrete manner in the world. It is an instruction that is often misunderstood by the character.

How should this instruction of healing manifest? What does it look like in real life? This is a quest that haunts her throughout her life. However, the urge to manifest this purpose is always prevalent, driving her to take the next step.

The other force is ascending. It has to do with the character's growth in awareness and consciousness. It holds the keys to unlock the creational energy available in every one of the seven energy consciousness planes. It is like climbing a ladder. Every rung of the ladder brings the character to another plane of awareness, consciousness, and energy flow. Where she finds herself, the consciousness plane on the ladder, determines how she interprets her mission on earth. The consciousness plane serves as a lens through which she translates her mission or purpose.

The ladder is the gateway to heaven. As she ascends the ladder, her growth in awareness matures into the *Christ consciousness*, if I may borrow the concept from my favorite author, Edgar Cayce. As she unlocks the creational energy of every plane, it becomes easier to descend and manifest her spiritual ideal or instruction in the world. She brings those planes of energy into the process of manifestation.

However, the main character in the movie chooses the hard way. She does not climb the ladder in easy strides. No, on every one of the seven planes, she gets off the ladder and wrestles through the drama and trauma on that specific plane. She struggles to see *the way*. And so, she fights the dragons of fear, grief, doubt, loss, lies, and delusion that emerge on every plane, and she translates her mission according to those lenses.

Tears roll down my cheeks. Deep sadness for the character threatens to overwhelm me. I watch her entering the first testing plane. At this stage, I know she is totally unaware of the reason she is experiencing so much pain. I am so overcome with emotion and sympathy that I almost want to shout that she will be OK. She will reach the top of the ladder. "Just make the right choice, little girl. It is easy," I hear myself saying out loud in the empty theater.

The movie is made in such a way that ascending is not an automatic given. The character can also descend at any time, depending on the choices she makes. There is nobody to help her, and she must figure this out for herself.

I watch the girl when she is still on the first plane. She is fourteen years old and struggling with the rejection of her community. I see her breaking through social conditioning and realizing that there is a deeper truth than what the community would want her to believe is true. She triumphs over this plane but is left with scars caused by mistrust, anger, and a deep feeling of detachment and separation.

I heave a deep sigh. Edgar Cayce described this feeling as the major sin of humanity. It is the feeling that you are alone, lost, and detached—almost like an uprooted tree, pulled with force from the soil. One must remember that soil is the first created element. Therefore, it is almost impossible to manifest a life ideal if one's roots are not firmly grounded in the earth.

How she gets it right, heaven alone knows, but the girl survives the first plane. Maybe it is her strong, stubborn, logical brain that carries her. She finds the ladder again and ascends to the second plane.

On this plane, the test is to measure how we flow through life. Life is a river, a stream of energy. If you stay in the energetic flow, trusting it completely, the energy will also flow through you. However, if you resist, trying to control the flow, your resistance will cause pain.

I watch the girl, now a young woman in the movie, wanting success so strongly that she makes two mistakes. She chases success at all costs and tries to control everything in her life. She goes faster and faster down the river. However, it is only an illusion, as the river wants her to believe she is sailing in the boat of success.

She is fighting the dragon of worth by trying to prove her own value through her achievements. She is still carrying the scars from the first plane. Through hard work and diligent dedication, she finds success in a masters and then a doctoral degree, qualifying as a psychologist. She achieves great things in the corporate world. But she remains oblivious to the fact that all these successes are not enough to feed the hungry dragon of self-worth.

Life, however, brings about balance and therefore throws her a curveball. If you continue to feed your own idea of your lack of worth, life will get you back to the river of truth and energy flow. At this river, everybody is worthy, and nobody is lacking. Qualifications and success will not compensate for lack of worth.

The only thing that will change it is her own inner sense that she was born with worth. She is already perfect for her mission. She lacks nothing. She just needs to flow with the river and stop trying to prove and to control. She might not be perfect as a person, but she is perfect for her own life mission.

Life decides to slow her down to teach her this principle. She survives a car accident and later is diagnosed with dystonia in her left foot. Only then does she realize she is resisting her own flow and overcome the dragons of grief, loss, and self-worth.

She triumphs over this consciousness plane—also the plane of the water element. The more she fights the dystonia, the more she experiences the effects, as if the river is blocked. When she relaxes and flows gently with the stream, she feels a positive movement, and the dystonia disappears. This becomes her life speedometer. Traveling at a leisurely pace down the river allows better appreciation of the scenery along the banks. She deserves this first-class seat on the boat of life.

*   *   *

From where I am sitting comfortably in my seat, I have to smile. There is such a paradox in thinking this way. Here we are told that the harder we try, the less we will achieve anything. Human nature usually does exactly the opposite!

I have noticed something else in the scene on plane two. When the woman was in a car accident, her little daughter was protected by angels, of which nobody was aware. But the woman realizes that her child was protected and keeps telling the little one that her angels were with her that day. At which the little girl asks, "Where were Mommy's angels? Why did Mommy get hurt?" She cannot answer that question yet. However, it does make her wonder.

As I watch, the woman climbs the ladder to plane three. The moment her feet touch down, fires start burning. This is the plane of power and will.

Why does this poor woman have to go through so many fires to triumph over the temptations on this plane? There are indeed a series of hellfires. My eyes, still glued to the screen, see the woman repeatedly making the same mistakes. Every mistake lights a new fire she needs to put out.

At some point, I want to shout at her, "Oh please, don't you get it? If you do that again, you will start another fire." Blindly, she keeps repeating the same actions again and again.

Sitting in my chair, I am exhausted on her behalf. Maybe it is true that we must first build character strength before we are able to carry our true power. Power is a huge responsibility. As is fire: we can cook food with fire but also burn down a whole city. When we find our true power, we can use it either to build or to destroy.

When the woman sees the effect of the power others have over her, she gains her own strength and rises to her own true power. Realizing what real power can do, she finds triumph on this plane. However, she is humbled by the fact that she is entrusted with such strength. Power is a strong creational energy. She is able to let things happen at her own will.

Following this scene, I grab my bottle of water and drink thirstily. It is as if I want to quench a hellfire burning inside me. I am exhausted and slightly nauseous, having watched the woman putting out one fire after the other on this plane. At one stage, I seriously thought she was going to fail, but she triumphed in the end.

*   *   *

The woman reaches for the ladder again and ascends to plane four. This is the heart plane, also associated with the element of air. After the hellfire of plane three, this one should be plain sailing, or maybe even plain breathing? But the contrary is true for our main character.

This plane is a divide in many ways. This is where the logical, rational brain starts to realize its own limitations. It slowly starts to acknowledge that the heart might, after all, hold some ancient wisdom worth listening to. On the screen, I watch as the woman discovers this intuitive gift we all possess.

With a sigh of relief, I see her starting to trust the gift of intuition, slowly realizing there is more than the eye can see. I feel her pain when she loses some wonderful friends, but this time her loss is different. Her previous losses were reinforced by her self-limiting belief of her separateness, of being alone and not good enough. In contrast, the losses on this fourth plane bring her closer to a realization of being part of something much bigger.

Attending her father-in-law's funeral, the woman reaches an understanding that what we leave behind when we die is not a legacy in something we have created but a legacy of woven relationships. We are put on earth for each other. We are all part of the breath of life, where we breathe together in rhythm. Or we can deprive ourselves of this freely available air and suffocate alone by choice.

On this plane, the woman finds a pearl of wisdom: *There is nothing to forgive. There are only coplayers in the story we call Life.*

I am witness to angels drying the woman's tears and healing her heart of sadness, grief, and loss. They replace the tears with seeds of gratitude. But because the angels are invisible to her, the woman thinks she did it all herself.

Slowly, the woman starts ascending the ladder to the fifth plane: the plane of truth, thought, and vibration. Here she has the realization that all of us are part of connected energy. This energy can vibrate, making it sensitive to the human voice. When the woman speaks her truth of who she really is, there is a distinct vibration noticeable. Because she is truthful and authentic, she can manifest with her voice, as in the promise, "Ask, and it will be given."

However, when not speaking the truth, energy will not react toward the false noise. The woman grows extremely sensitive to the subtle and invisible energy and possibility. It is as if a gentle hand guides her toward favoring truth in her life choices. It includes the truth about her purpose, the truth about others, and the truth about just causes.

Her emotions start to function as her compass, immediately showing her when something is off-beat or off-resonance. She also learns that on some occasions, you will be the coplayer in somebody else's journey, and then the lesson is not for you. It is almost as if you repay an uncomfortable favor to a friend. This all happens in the name of balancing energy and creating resonance.

The screen suddenly goes black. At first, I think it is the end of the movie, but then I realize it is probably just an interval. This was part one, and more will follow.

Using the break to stretch my legs, I reflect on the first part of the movie. It seems the ascending force intends to purify and awaken latent creational energy. Once this energy has been fully charged, the character becomes quite powerful. It is almost like teaching a young person to drive a car. It has a powerful engine, but you need to obey rules and regulations when driving in order to be safe. Otherwise, the power could cause injury or even death.

Maybe that is why Jacob was in such a state of shock after waking up from his dream. He had seen this latent power in people. He knew that the more aware we become, the more powerful we are.

CHAPTER 18

A Moment in the Theatre, Part Two

As the screen starts to flicker, I return to my seat to watch the next part. But there must be some technical glitch, as the screen goes dark again. I sink deeper into my chair and think about the movie so far.

I start thinking about the descending part of the character's *souljourn*—a journey of the soul indeed. The descending force wants to demonstrate something concrete in the world. The spark of magic makes the world a better place and leaves evidence thereof long after the soul has journeyed back to its source.

Edgar Cayce always referred to the mind as the builder of our realities. The body provides energy and the material to build, but the mind must provide the ideal of what to build— like a blueprint for a house plan. In the first part of the movie, I watched the woman receive a calling to do something concrete in the world. She refers to it as "healing," linking with the Biblical calling to "heal the sick ... tell the people the Kingdom is near or within you."

Still waiting for the theater to sort out the technical problem and the movie to continue, I contemplate the character's journey of discovery.

Her whole life journey shows evidence of invitations to display her calling to heal. It is almost as if life leaves small invitations everywhere to all of us to remind and invite us to demonstrate our purpose.

Imagine that this is true for us all—that there is a point before we are born and our life movie starts where we agree to the mission or calling of our lives. To make the interconnected world the amazing place it is meant to be, we all agree to a different but very specific vocation. Each of us is a different expression of that greatness. We are all a unique and holy ideal breathed into existence, ready to manifest that promise, something we are constantly reminded of.

Is it not true that we all have a sense of that ideal? Are not all of us searching for it, like the main character in this movie? Are not all of us following the invitations, almost laid out like a trail of breadcrumbs for us? And don't we all wonder if it will eventually lead to our reason for existence?

I look back on the breadcrumb trail laid for our main character. It provides very specific pause points in her life. She starts off on a lonely quest, following a hero's journey of her own. This is already a clear invitation to her curious, sharp brain to investigate possibilities of something more to discover. Nobody will go on a journey if the soul is not restless. The soul needs to yearn for something worthy, something more to explore. This is true for the woman in the movie. Maybe the restlessness of the soul is the first sign life sends us to start us on our journey.

But as with any fairy tale, the hero needs a special gift or power. It can be something physical to hold on to or something handy to use on life's journey—as Thor had his hammer.

The woman in our movie has the precious gift of books. From an early age, life has generously provided her with this powerful tool. This gift will guide her whole life. Her relationship with books is truly unique—a hero's superpower. It might also be how the angels talk to her, because they see that she trusts books to guide her. It takes time before she recognizes her gift, but she embraces it with abandon when she does.

I believe all humans should have a superpower to support their life ideas. But how many people know they should search for their superpower, and how many find it?

However, a yearning and a superpower will not be enough to send our main character on her life journey. She will need a gentle push and a lot of courage. In the story, a helper steps in to act as a guide and plants the idea that she should see and unlock potential in others. This happens when a colleague shows her how good she is at guiding people to recognize their own purpose and potential. He explains that her *true being and identity* are her gift to others. By helping other people find their purpose, she helps them in their healing journey. Knowing this, she finds the courage to continue to pursue this possibility.

It is so easy not to understand that we are able to heal others when we present our true selves to them. How do we find our true selves and our true ideals, and when we do, why do we lack the courage to act on that? Or are we just paralyzed by fear that we might never find our true selves and our true nature?

I guess once a hero has a yearning, a superpower, and courage, the timing is perfect for embarking on an actual journey. When the soul is restless and wants to answer the intense calling, the hero will set out on the journey.

Once, I was brave enough to volunteer to join some friends on a hiking trail. The first day was full of excitement and laughter, but it was harder and harder to keep up as the days went by. My backpack was chafing, my legs were tired, my muscles were aching, and somewhere along the way, my mind started playing tricks on me. I kept hearing a voice trying to convince me that the hiking trip was an insane idea. When the body hurts and the mind wants to keep the body safe and end the ordeal, it is easy to forget the soul's calling.

What would be a better solution than to give an explicit *instruction* to the hero? And what could be more precise than *heal the sick* and *write it down?* However, when we are on our life journey, things are not always clear and easy. Maybe it is because of all the destruction and trauma along the way, or perhaps it is just tiredness. Whatever the case, it is so easy to miss the punchline of the instructions.

Maybe it will help to send a teacher. Our main character eventually needs two teachers to make the vision clear to her. Only then does she grasp the instruction's true meaning and realize that she needs to write her life lessons in a book. This is the point at which she finally understands the expectations of the exact concrete mission ahead of her. The teachers literally spell it out for her: *This is what you must do, and this is how. Healing will happen through the book you will write. There is no other way to fulfill the promise.*

Why can we not just run off and fulfill the promise any way we want to? Why must we learn an exact technique at all? Because not only does the woman receive her mission, but she is also told exactly how to fulfill it. She is not only to write her teachings down, but she also needs to write them down in a specific way. Apparently, the *angle* and the *perspective* are more important than she has thought.

The discipline and the neatness are equally important. The details matter to the Universe! The character becomes aware that there is more to the theory than what she initially has perceived. She starts seeing her own limiting belief patterns, as well as the patterns of the life lessons.

She notices that she needs to climb the ladder from the bottom up, and on each plane, she needs to unlock and purify the creational energy, the energy needed to fulfill her mission.

She must clear every consciousness plane by slaying the dragons that lie there disguised as beliefs. It is necessary to kill the dragon that presides over each plane in order to reach the ultimate prize. On every plane, she recognizes each dragon for what it is. The most important trick the dragons use is to try to hypnotize her to remain on a specific plane.

The dragons want her to fall asleep on a particular consciousness plane. On every plane, the dragon uses a soothing lullaby to rock her into a guileless sleep, unable to heed her calling. There are different pacifying lullabies for the brain, the body, and emotions, all aimed at keeping her away from the ladder. But softly, in the background, she hears the murmuring voices of teachers and mentors. She also still receives the precious gift of various books to wake her from her slumbers.

And so, she manages to slay the dragon and can grab the ladder to continue her climb—only to find a new dragon singing lullabies on the next plane. With every conquest, she gains more wisdom, power, and creational energy. Most importantly, she becomes immune to the soothing sounds of lullabies.

With every rung she climbs, she learns more about the ladder: ascend with discipline and do not linger on a plane that gives the dragon a chance to hypnotize you. There is only one force that should lift you up. It is the force of love and not of fear. It is fear that makes one hear lullabies.

Sudden flickers on the movie screen bring me back from my reverie. I have lost track of time while reflecting on the points of the woman's journey so far. What more will follow now?

CHAPTER 19

A Moment in the Theatre, Part Three

When there is more flickering on the screen, I realize the movie is about to start. The main character was left on plane five when the movie stopped earlier. Now she ascends to plane six. This is the element of light and vision. It is interesting to note that the character has changed. When asked what she wants to learn on this plane, fully aware now that she may do so, she asks to see miracles!

At first, I think the woman has lost the plot. But then it starts to make sense to me. If she intuitively knows she is ascending the ladder, miracles are such a clever thing to ask for.

The character is practicing intuitive visioning capability. If she can see the small miracles when the whole world is suffering from the worldwide virus pandemic, she will be able to strengthen her belief that there is always more than meets the eye. It is an inner knowing and wisdom.

Despite the daily insanity and bad news, she feeds on everything happening in the world, and she wants to believe there is another truth. If she can see small miracles, she will also be able to see patterns, connections, and eventually the whole web.

Then, when she can see the web, she will ascend to plane seven. She is aware that everything is connected. We are one organism, connected by the Akashic field. There is great intelligence present in this field. Once the woman acknowledges the existence of this field, she has no fear, no grief, no anger, no sadness, no lies, and no delusions.

Being human, she understands she will descend to the lower planes from time to time. Again, she will have to fight the dragons of fear, grief, anger, loss, lies, and delusion. But now she knows about Akasha. She is from this field; she is in the field, and the field is in her. She is the field. She realizes that this is consciousness in its purest form. This field is pure love. This is the God plane.

This is the perspective from which she can fulfill her calling to "write the ladder on clay tablets." When she stands on the seventh rung, she can see all the other rungs beneath her. Also visible are the seven planes, where one can dwell and get hypnotized by the dragons and fall into oblivious sleep.

Interestingly, when she looks down, she notices there have been nine points of pause on her journey. Maybe these have been points where she was prepared for her mission. These were invitation points where life called for her to pause and helped her prepare for her life mission—one can call them *purpose pause points.*

She knows now when she arrives safely on plane seven, she will see her life mission from the perspective of ultimate love and can descend the ladder with the intent to live her mission—showing that love in its purest form. At its core, all missions intend to connect us in love and to this love.

She knows not to get hypnotized by lullabies, because that might prevent her pure manifestation. Even worse, she might display an illusion, as suggested by the dragon's lullaby. A mission influenced by a lullaby might contain elements of fear, grief, anger, sadness, and delusion.

Now she recognizes everything for what it is. She writes all she has experienced and learned on clay tablets and slowly descends the ladder to announce and declare her teachings to all. The time has arrived to teach others about *The Ladder of Jacob*.

The woman reaches the conclusion that healing is both an ascending and descending force. Suddenly, the idea of Jacob's ladder makes so much sense. Writing down all the lessons and recollections, she heals herself with every letter that appears on paper. She is ready to publish her book.

Beautiful music starts playing as the last image on the screen flickers away—the end of the movie. I take a moment to reflect on the woman's healing. Is that why we all are here on earth? To heal every part of our souls?

We teach best, what we most need to learn. Richard Bach's words echo in my head.

I slowly start to climb the ladder in my mind again.

To the seventh plane.

The God plane.

Jacob's dream from Genesis 28:16-17 slowly plays in my head again: "Then Jacob awoke from his sleep and said, 'Surely the Lord is in this place, and I wasn't even aware of it! ... What an awesome place this is! It is none other than the house of God, the very gateway to heaven!'"

As the music fades out, the lights in the theater go up. A door opens at the front of the theatre, and an old man walks toward me. He is dressed in a snow-white linen tunic, his hair the grey of a rainy sky. As he draws nearer, our eyes meet. His deep blue eyes reflect wisdom. When he speaks, his deep voice resonates in every cell of my body.

"Is there anything that you would like to change in this story?" he asks.

151

I am almost too tired to speak; my voice is a soft murmur. Watching the movie has drained me, both emotionally and physically.

"No, I think it is perfect," I manage in a hoarse whisper.

There is a knowing in his eyes, the same knowing I saw in my friend Anna's eyes all those years ago.

I slowly get out of my seat to leave the theater.

The man's voice reverberates again. "You know you are privileged to have seen this movie?"

"Yes," my tired voice replies.

Realizing that it is time to leave, I start walking toward the back of the theater. I feel a gentle hand on my back, guiding me towards the exit.

At first, I notice the guidance is firm yet tender, but then I also recognize it as familiar—as if I have felt it before.

When I open the theater door, the hand is gone, and I walk outside into the sunshine.

I remember the warm smile on the wise man's face.

I am loved.

As I step outside into the sundrenched street, I cannot help but think of Jacob.

"Surely the Lord is in this place, and I wasn't even aware of it! ... What an awesome place this is! It is none other than the house of God, the very gateway to heaven!"

Bibliography

Amen, D. G. *Change Your Brain, Change Your Life: The Breakthrough Program for Conquering Anxiety, Depression, Obsessiveness, Anger, and Impulsiveness.* New York: Three Rivers Press, 1998.

Bach, R. *Illusions: The Adventures of a Reluctant Messiah.* London: Pan Books Ltd., 1978.

Barnett, E. A. *Unlock Your Mind and Be Free! A Practical Approach to Hypnotherapy.* Kingston, Ontario, Canada: Junica Publishing Company Limited, 2005.

Barrett, R. *What My Soul Told Me: A Practical Guide to Soul Activation.* Bath, UK: Fulfilling Books, 2012.

Baxter, P., and Jack, S. "Qualitative Case Study Methodology: Study Design and Implementation for Novice Researchers." *The Qualitative Report* 13, no. 4 (December 2008): 544–559.

Bernstein, G. *The Universe Has Your Back: Transform Fear to Faith.* New York, USA: Hay House, Inc., 2016.

Braden, G. *The Divine Matrix: Bridging Time, Space, Miracles, and Belief.* New York, USA: Hay House, Inc., 2007.

Byrne, L. *Angels in My Hair.* Kent: Cornerstone Digital, 2008 (revised ed.).

———. *Angels at My Fingertips: The Sequel to Angels in My Hair: How Angels and Our Loved Ones Help Guide Us.* London: Coronet Books, 2017.

Chestnut, B. *The Complete Enneagram: 27 Paths to Greater Self-Knowledge.* Berkeley, USA: She Writes Press, 2013.

Chopra, D. *Quantum Healing: Exploring the Frontiers of Mind/Body Medicine.* New York: Bantam Books, 1998.

Church, D. *Mind to Matter: The Astonishing Science of How Your Brain Creates Material Reality.* New York, USA: Hay House, Inc., 2018.

Cloete, D. *Integrative Enneagram for Practitioners.* Cape Town, South Africa: ABC Press, 2019.

Coelho, P. *The Alchemist.* London: Harper Collins Publishers, 1992.

Dahlitz, M. *The Psychotherapist's Essential Guide to the Brain.* Park Ridge, Queensland, Australia: Dahlitz Media, 2017.

Emoto, M. *The Hidden Messages in Water.* New York, USA: Atria Books, 2011.

Engler, B. *Personality Theories: An Introduction.* Boston: Houghton Mifflin Company, 1985.

Farias, J. *Intertwined: How to Induce Neuroplasticity—A New Approach to Rehabilitating Dystonias.* Galene Editions, 2012.

Feige, K. (producer) and K. Branagh (director). *Thor.* USA: Marvel Studios, 2011.

Frankl, V. E. *Man's Search for Meaning.* New York: Washington Square Press Publication, 1984.

Goddard, N. *The Power of Awareness.* USA: Road to Success, 2019 (special Kindle ed.).

Goldberg, E. *The New Executive Brain: Frontal Lobes in a Complex World.* New York: Oxford University Press, 2009.

Hay, L. *You Can Heal Your Life.* New York, USA: Hay House, Inc., 2010.

Judith, A. *Eastern Body Western Mind: Psychology and the Chakra System as a Path to the Self.* New York: Crown Publishing Group. 2004.

———. *Wheels of Life: A User's Guide to the Chakra System.* Woodbury, Minnesota: Llewellyn Publications, 2015.

László, E. *Science and the Akashic Field: An Integral Theory of Everything.* USA: Lake Book Manufacturing, Inc., 2007.

Ledwell, N. *Never in Your Wildest Dreams. A Transformational Story to Tap Into Your Hidden Gifts to Create a Life of Passion, Purpose, and Prosperity.* Cheyenne, Wyoming: Sherpa Press, 2013.

Lipton, B. H. *The Biology of Belief: Unleashing the Power of Consciousness, Matter, and Miracles.* New York, USA: Hay House, Inc., 2005.

Matthee, D. *Kringe in 'n Bos.* ("Circles in a Forest"). Cape Town: Tafelberg-Uitgewers Beperk, 1994.

Moorjani, A. *Dying to Be Me: My Journey from Cancer, to Near Death, to True Healing.* New York, USA: Hay House, Inc., 2012.

Munroe, M. *In Pursuit of Purpose.* USA: Destiny Image Publishers, Inc., 1992.

Myss, C. *Anatomy of the Spirit. The Seven Stages of Power and Healing.* London: Bantam Books, 1997.

———. *Defy Gravity: Healing Beyond the Bounds of Reason.* New York, USA: Hay House, Inc., 2009.

Ortner, N. *The Tapping Solution: A Revolutionary System for Stress-Free Living.* New York, USA: Hay House, Inc., 2013.

Pert, C. B. *Molecules of Emotion: The Science Behind Mind-Body Medicine.* New York: Scribner, 2010.

Puryear, H. B. *A Psychology of the Soul: From the Infinite into the Finite.* Fort St, Victoria, Canada: FriesenPress, 2020.

Quote Investigator. "The truth will set you free." https://quoteinvestigator.com/2014/09/04/truth-free/.

Researchgate.net. "Autoethnography defined by Garance Maréchal (2010)." https://www.researchgate.net/publication/301551651_Autoethnography.

Rydall, D. *Emergence: Seven Steps for Radical Life Change.* New York, USA: Atria Books/Beyond Words, 2015.

Scarlett, H. *Neuroscience for Organisational Change: An Evidence-Based Practical Guide to Managing Change.* London: Kogan Page, 2019.

Seaman, T. *Diagnosis Dystonia: Navigating the Journey.* Wilmington, North Carolina, USA: Shadow Panther Press, 2015.

Sharma, R. S. *The Monk Who Sold His Ferrari: A Spiritual Fable about Fulfilling Your Dreams and Reaching Your Destiny.* London: Harper Collins Publishers, 1997.

Smit, H. *Beneath: Exploring the Unconscious in Individuals.* South Africa: Moonshine Media, 2011.

Strassman, R. *DMT: The Spirit Molecule: A Doctor's Revolutionary Research into the Biology of Near-Death and Mystical Experiences.* Rochester, Vermont, USA: Park Street Press, 2000.

Sugrue, T. J. *There Is a River: The Story of Edgar Cayce.* New York: TarcherPerigee, 2015.

Todeschi, K. J. *Edgar Cayce on the Akashic Records.* Virginia Beach, Virginia: A.R.E. Press., 1998.

Tolle, E. *A New Earth: Awakening to Your Life's Purpose.* London: Penguin Books Ltd., 2005.

Van Auken, J. *Edgar Cayce's Amazing Interpretation of the Revelation.* Virginia Beach, Virginia: Living in the Light, 2015.

———. *Edgar Cayce on the Spiritual Forces Within You: Unlock Your Soul with: Dreams, Intuition, Kundalini, and Meditation.* Virginia Beach, Virginia: A.R.E. Press, 2014.

Wikipedia. "Jellyfish." https://en.wikipedia.org/wiki/Jellyfish.

Wise, A. *Awakening the Mind. A Guide to Mastering the Power of Your Brain Waves.* New York: Penguin Group (USA) Inc., 2002.

Ziskin, L., and I. Bryce (producers), S. Raimi (director), *Spider-Man.* Based on *Spider-Man* by S. Lee and S. Ditko. USA: Marvel Studios, 2002.

Zukav, G. *The Seat of the Soul: An Inspiring Vision of Humanity's Spiritual Destiny.* London: Ebury Digital, 2012.

Printed in the United States
by Baker & Taylor Publisher Services

essentials

essentials liefern aktuelles Wissen in konzentrierter Form. Die Essenz dessen, worauf es als „State-of-the-Art" in der gegenwärtigen Fachdiskussion oder in der Praxis ankommt. *essentials* informieren schnell, unkompliziert und verständlich

- als Einführung in ein aktuelles Thema aus Ihrem Fachgebiet
- als Einstieg in ein für Sie noch unbekanntes Themenfeld
- als Einblick, um zum Thema mitreden zu können

Die Bücher in elektronischer und gedruckter Form bringen das Expertenwissen von Springer-Fachautoren kompakt zur Darstellung. Sie sind besonders für die Nutzung als eBook auf Tablet-PCs, eBook-Readern und Smartphones geeignet. *essentials:* Wissensbausteine aus den Wirtschafts-, Sozial- und Geisteswissenschaften, aus Technik und Naturwissenschaften sowie aus Medizin, Psychologie und Gesundheitsberufen. Von renommierten Autoren aller Springer-Verlagsmarken.

Weitere Bände in der Reihe http://www.springer.com/series/13088

Stefan Schmid

Was Sie im Alltag von Soldaten lernen können

Mit simplen Techniken leichter
durchs Leben

Springer Gabler

Stefan Schmid
Olching, Deutschland

ISSN 2197-6708   ISSN 2197-6716   (electronic)
essentials
ISBN 978-3-658-27761-1   ISBN 978-3-658-27762-8   (eBook)
https://doi.org/10.1007/978-3-658-27762-8

Die Deutsche Nationalbibliothek verzeichnet diese Publikation in der Deutschen Nationalbibliografie; detaillierte bibliografische Daten sind im Internet über http://dnb.d-nb.de abrufbar.

Springer Gabler ist ein Imprint der eingetragenen Gesellschaft Springer Fachmedien Wiesbaden
GmbH und ist ein Teil von Springer Nature.
Die Anschrift der Gesellschaft ist: Abraham-Lincoln-Str. 46, 65189 Wiesbaden, Germany

Was Sie in diesem *essential* finden können

- Einen Ansatz Probleme zu lösen, der seine Grundlage in der militärischen Lagebeurteilung hat.
- Die praxisorientierte Kombination populärer Managementtechniken mit militärischen Grundsätzen.
- Eine einfache Strategie, die bei nahezu allen Problemen einen Lösungsansatz aufzeigt.
- Ein praktisches Beispiel, das zeigt, wie eine simple Problemstellung theoretisch und zügig angegangen werden kann.

Vorwort

Dieses *essential* ist nicht wissenschaftlich, sondern im wahrsten Sinne des Wortes, ein Praxisleitfaden. Alles was darin steht, hat bereits wiederholt funktioniert. Aber natürlich sind auch theoretische Grundlagen eingeflossen, die allerdings aus Bereichen kommen, die sich nicht nur unterscheiden, sondern in unterschiedlichen Welten zu liegen scheinen.

Verschiedene Welten

Die unterschiedlichen Welten sind dabei durch scheinbar unüberwindliche Mauern voneinander getrennt und wollen herzlich wenig voneinander wissen: Zivilleben und Militär. Verständlicherweise und aufgrund unserer Geschichte ist diese Trennung gerade in Deutschland besonders ausgeprägt. Die Aussetzung der Wehrplicht hat ein Übriges dazu getan, sie zu manifestieren, denn sie entfernt die Bundeswehr nicht unwesentlich aus dem zivilen Bewusstsein. Wie überall, so führt auch hier strikte Abgrenzung zu Vorurteilen: Dann wird alles Militärische als stumpf, zackig und wenig effektiv abgetan. Ähnlich passiert es ja auch oft mit anderen Disziplinen: Alles was mit Psychologie zu tun hat, wird als weich, esoterisch und ineffektiv empfunden. Die Kreativbranche besteht aus unstrukturierten Chaoten und Betriebswirte sind zahlenhörige Bürokraten, die in Excel-Tabellen denken und ohnehin nur auf Personaleinsparungen aus sind. In Deutschland existiert für all die genannten Disziplinen Fachliteratur. Allerdings ist auch die sauber getrennt. Literatur, die moderne Managementinhalte, Psychologie und militärische Inhalte zusammenbringt ist nicht zu finden. Stattdessen schreiben die Autoren militärischer Inhalte wie Soldaten für Soldaten, Wirtschaftswissenschaftler meist theoretisch-trocken für Betriebswirte und Psychologen wissenschaftlich kompliziert für andere Psychologen und Pädagogen. Das wiederum trägt dazu bei, Vorurteile zu bestätigen, Mauern nur höher zu ziehen und somit nicht voneinander zu lernen. Das ist schade, denn genau in ihrer Kombination entfalten die jeweiligen Inhalte ihren praktischen Nutzen und damit ihre Stärke. Als unsoldatischer Ex-Soldat, leidenschaftsloser Betriebswirt, erfahrener und psychologisch weitergebildeter Kommunikationsmanager versuche ich hier, genau diesen Mehrwert zu bieten.

Zusammen, was nicht zusammengehört

Also bringe ich Tipps und Tricks aus Bereichen zusammen, die ansonsten kaum zusammenkommen: militärischer Taktik, Kommunikation, Psychologie, Betriebswirtschaftslehre, aber auch aus dem Leistungssport. Das alles lässt eine Toolbox entstehen, aus der Sie sich bedienen können. Manche Werkzeuge passen vielleicht auch auf Ihr Problem, andere tun das gegebenenfalls nicht. Sie können Teile daraus mit Ihren eigenen Prinzipien kombinieren und somit Ihre eigenen Strategien und Taktiken entwickeln. Wie dabei nicht ungewöhnlich, werden Sie das ein oder andere schon längst gewusst, aber vielleicht trotzdem nie beachtet haben. Schon damit hätte dieses *essential* einen ersten Mehrwert erreicht, indem es vermeintliche Selbstverständlichkeiten ausspricht und somit den Scheinwerfer auf sie richtet.

Die Zielgruppe

Die Inhalte dieses *essentials* dürften jedem weiterhelfen. Das macht es schwer, eine bestimmte Zielgruppe zu beschreiben. Im Arbeitsalltag fallen mir ständig Kolleginnen und Kollegen auf, die davon profitieren könnten – trotz ihrer erstklassigen fachlichen Ausbildung. Das gleiche gilt für Verwandte und manche oder manchen in meinem Bekanntenkreis.

Der Aufbau des *essentials*

Wer sein Berufsleben in Uniform startet, vielleicht eine Ausbildung zum Offizier absolviert, der hat Grundlagen taktischer und strategischer Planung gelernt – in Theorie und in Praxis, die ihn sein ganzes Leben begleiten, auch außerhalb des Militärs. Also beginnt das Buch genau hier, wo die Grundlagen der behandelten Vorgehenssystematik liegen: im Militär. Das wir dabei von der Bundeswehr sprechen ist reiner Zufall, es könnte genauso gut jede andere Armee sein. Militär arbeitet meist ähnlich und geht in ähnlichen Schritten vor. Das *essential* nimmt sie als Basis und reichert sie mit zivilen Tipps und Vorgehensgrundsätzen an.

Stefan Schmid

Inhaltsverzeichnis

Über den Autor

Stefan Schmid sammelte 14 Jahre lang nationale und internationale Erfahrung als Offizier der Bundeswehr. Nach seinem Ausscheiden war er rund 10 Jahre Führungskraft in der Unternehmenskommunikation eines großen deutschen Nutzfahrzeugherstellers. Aktuell berät er hauptberuflich den Geschäftsführer eines kommunalen Unternehmens in allen Fragen rund um Kommunikation und arbeitet nebenher als freier Autor und Kommunikationsberater.

Probleme zu lösen ist nichts Ungewöhnliches, denn sie sind an der Tagesordnung. Im Grunde genommen, sind sie nur eine Veränderung des Ablaufes entgegen der Erwartung. Ob das dann ein Problem darstellt, hängt von der individuellen Interpretation ab. Da in einem immer komplexer werdenden Alltag viele Faktoren zusammenwirken, die sich immer weniger vorab erahnen lassen, treten Probleme entsprechend häufig, eigentlich ständig auf. Dabei kommt es nicht nur oft anders als man es erwartet hat, sondern in der Regel auch noch selten so, wie man es gerne nicht hätte und es somit als Hindernis empfindet (Problem: aus dem Griechischen „das Hingeworfene"). Mit diesem Umstand umzugehen, wiederholt sich unzählige Male im Leben. Umso erstaunlicher ist es, dass viele von uns trotzdem wenig zielgerichtet und systematisch reagieren und in der Folge schnell überfordert sind. Dabei, so unterschiedlich Probleme auch sein mögen, ein gewisses Muster ist immer zu erkennen. Wieso sollte man sich also nicht darauf einstellen, mit ihm umgehen und sich das Leben dadurch erheblich erleichtern?

Erkennbare Muster
Bei Problemen gibt es ein Vorhaben oder einen Sachverhalt, dessen normalen Ablauf etwas im Wege steht oder das dem Ablauf eine neue Richtung gibt. Dieses Etwas erfordert besondere Aufmerksamkeit, damit das Vorhaben oder der Sachverhalt wieder seinen beabsichtigten Verlauf nehmen kann. Meist spielen dabei verschiedene Dinge eine Rolle und es entsteht ein größerer Gesamtzusammenhang, den man im Auge haben sollte. Probleme können einfach oder komplexer sein, sie können auch auf den ersten Blick unlösbar erscheinen. Entwirrt man sie und gräbt etwas unter ihre Oberfläche, legt man damit immer das gleiche Muster frei. Und das ist relativ simpel.

© Springer Fachmedien Wiesbaden GmbH, ein Teil von Springer Nature 2020
S. Schmid, *Was Sie im Alltag von Soldaten lernen können*, essentials,
https://doi.org/10.1007/978-3-658-27762-8_1

Einfache Strategien

Also liegt es nahe, sich einen Fahrplan – ein Konzept – eine Strategie zurecht zu legen und somit Probleme anzugehen. Was tun wir stattdessen häufig? Wir verfallen entweder in Aktionismus, der zu Chaos führt, wollen viel und erreichen doch wenig. Oder wir werden zum Spielball der auftretenden Probleme, verlieren durch Passivität unsere Richtung oder finden sie erst gar nicht. Das passiert im Alltag genauso, wie den vermeintlichen Profis, die in Unternehmen jeglicher Größe arbeiten und deren Job es eigentlich ist, Dinge umzusetzen und Ziele strukturiert zu erreichen. Überraschend vieles passiert hier relativ kopflos, klappt zufällig oder eben nicht. Es werden Projekte aufgesetzt, Arbeitspakete geschnürt, Meilensteine festgelegt und nicht selten sind Projektstruktur und Systematik komplizierter als das eigentliche Problem und verstellen damit den klaren Blick auf dessen Lösung.

Militär

2

> **Was Sie in diesem Kapitel finden können**
>
> - Die Beschreibung der militärischen Kernaufgabe
> - Die Bedeutung festgelegter Routinen
> - Den grundlegenden Mehrwert von Initiative

Die Wurzeln dieses Buches sind grün. D. h. nicht, dass sie besonders neu wären, sondern dass sie im Militär liegen. Viele Soldaten, im Speziellen Offiziere, erlernen hier Inhalte und machen Erfahrungen, von denen sie ihr ganzes Leben lang profitieren. Denn ihre Ausbildung ist vielseitig, anspruchsvoll und dabei sehr systematisch und fundiert. Leider verstellen Klischee-Vorstellungen von exzessiven Trinkgelagen, schikanösen Ausbildern und stumpfen Befehl und Gehorsam zumeist den Blick darauf (Abb. 2.1). Daneben gibt es in weiten Teilen der deutschen Bevölkerung eine flammende Abneigung gegen alles Militärische – was bei der deutschen Vergangenheit nicht weiter überrascht und sicherlich auch seine Berechtigung hat. Macht man sich davon frei, lässt sich schnell erkennen, um was es bei der Ausbildung zum Soldaten oder zum Offizier im Kern geht: chaotische Situationen beherrschen und absolut Unübersichtliches überblicken. Dabei hilft strukturiertes Vorgehen. Einfach, robust, sodass es auch unter Belastung standhält. Vergleichbares gibt es auch im Rettungsdienst oder bei der Feuerwehr. Auch helfen festgelegte Algorithmen Rettungskräften dabei, kontrolliert zu agieren, auch wenn es drunter und drüber geht. Mit genau diesen werden auch

S. Schmid, *Was Sie im Alltag von Soldaten lernen können*, essentials,
https://doi.org/10.1007/978-3-658-27762-8_2

Abb. 2.1 So sieht es aus:
Das Klischee von Befehl
und Gehorsam

junge Offiziersanwärter getriezt. Sie arbeiten mit Aufträgen, werten Situationen anhand eines Schemas der Lagebeurteilung aus und formulieren daraufhin einen strukturierten Befehl an ihre unterstellten Soldaten. Mit festgelegten Vorgehensweisen ordnen sie relativ unübersichtliche Situationen und arbeiten einzelne Schritte sauber und diszipliniert nacheinander ab.

Hintergrundinformation
Die Grundlage, um militärische Lagen zu beurteilen, kommen unter anderem aus der Heeresdienstvorschrift Führung im Gefecht 100/100:

1. Auswertung des Auftrages
   – Absicht der übergeordneten Führung
   – Wesentliche Leistung
   – Auflagen für das eigene Handeln
   – Grundlegende Lageänderungen
   – Handlungsbedarf
   – Prüffragen
2. Beurteilung des Geländes und weiterer Umweltbedingungen
   – Allgemeine Charakteristik des Geländes
   – Abschnittsweise Beurteilung
   – Folgerungen für das Handeln des Feindes und das eigene Handeln
3. Beurteilung der Feindlage
   – Handlungsmöglichkeiten
   – Vermutete Absicht
   – Vermutete weitere Gefechtsführung
   – Folgerungen für das eigene Handeln

4. Beurteilung der eigenen Lage
   – Kampfkraft
   – Folgerungen für besondere Fähigkeiten, Einschränkungen der Handlungsfreiheit, Möglichkeiten des eigenen Handelns
5. Kräftevergleich
   – Kampfkraftvergleich
   – Gefechtswert
   – Folgerungen für das Gesetz des Handelns, Taktische Gesamtabsicht, Möglichkeiten des eigenen Handelns
6. Möglichkeiten des Handelns (nach Gefechtsphasen)
   – Feststellen gemeinsamer Elemente (der Möglichkeiten)
   – Kampfkraftvergleich
   – Vor- und Nachteile
   – Abwägen

Das Schema funktioniert dabei als Weg, der über seine einzelnen Stationen systematisch zu den möglichen Handlungsalternativen führt.

Die Einschätzung der Situation, die Lagebeurteilung und der daraus resultierende Befehl können dabei ausführlich formuliert sein oder aber sehr knapp ausfallen. Das ist abhängig von der jeweiligen Situation und dem zur Verfügung stehenden Zeitbedarf. Grundlage für die Formulierung des Befehls ist auch ein Schema, das nach einem standardisierten Abkommen gleichermaßen für alle Armeen der NATO-Staaten gilt.

Hintergrundinformation
Befehlsschema, gültig für alle NATO-Staaten (Heeresdienstvorschrift 100/200 Führungssystem des Heeres):
   Lage

* Feind (Stärke, Art, Verhalten, vermutete Absicht)
* Eigene Lage (Lage, Auftrag und Absicht des übergeordneten Truppenteils)
* Unterstellungen und Abgaben (Soldaten, die on anderen Truppenteilen temporär zugeordnet wurden)
* Zivilisten (wo sind ggf. noch Zivilisten anwesend, besteht Gefahrenpotenzial?)

Auftrag

* Knappe Darlegung des eigenen Auftrags
* Durchführung
* Eigene Absicht mit geplanter Operationsführung
* Aufträge an die unterstellten Truppen
* Sicherung und Gefechtsfeldaufklärung

ABC-Abwehr

- Fliegerabwehr/Flugabwehr
- Maßnahmen zur Koordinierung (z. B. Anmarsch)
- Einsatzunterstützung
- Wichtige Maßnahmen und Einrichtungen der Versorgung

Führung und Fernmeldewesen

- Einzelheiten zum Funkverkehr, Erkennungszeichen, Platz des Gefechtsstandes (der Operationszentrale)

Die standardisierte Gliederung erleichtert es, kein Detail zu vergessen und lückenlos und effizient die eigene Absicht zu vermitteln. Gleichzeitig zwingt sie zu Ruhe und Konzentration. Denn die Arbeit eines Soldaten spielt sich gewöhnlich nicht am Schreibtisch ab, sondern im Gelände, womöglich sogar unter Beschuss und im absoluten Chaos (Abb. 2.2). Also lernen junge Offiziere, mit Informationsflut umzugehen. Sie lernen aus vielen belanglosen Details, Wichtiges herauszufiltern, sich dabei nicht aus der Ruhe bringen zu lassen und den Blick fürs Wesentliche nicht zu verlieren. Standardisierte Vorgehensroutinen erleichtern das wesentlich, denn sie beantworten zumindest schon mal die Frage der ersten Vorgehensweise. Das alles wird in der Ausbildung mit körperlicher Belastung, Schlafmangel, Hunger und Durst kombiniert. Schon in der Ausbildung sind Stress, ständig wechselnde Situationen und das Missverhältnis zwischen

Abb. 2.2 Gefechtssituationen haben eines gemeinsam: den fehlenden Überblick

unvollständiger Information einerseits und einer verwirrenden Informationsflut andererseits, ganz wesentliche Kernelemente.

Struktur hilft

Struktur ist etwas Gutes. Wie so oft im Leben, kann man es natürlich auch mit ihr übertreiben. Dann führt sie zu übertriebener Statik und macht unbeweglich. Richtig eingesetzt, verschafft sie allerdings Ordnung. Also lernen junge Offiziersanwärter, sich mit ihren Taschenkarten an zahlreichen Akronymen und vorgegebenen Schemen zu orientieren, um Situationen zu beurteilen und Befehle zu formulieren. Die ständig wiederkehrenden Abläufe gehen sehr schnell in Fleisch und Blut über. Zwangsläufig, denn Übungs- und Gefechtssituationen machen es natürlich unmöglich, mit Merkzettel, respektive Taschenkarte vor der Nase herumzulaufen. Lage – Auftrag – Durchführung: Oft ist es dieser simple Dreiklang, der hilft, Situationen zu beurteilen und auf dieser Basis Entscheidungen in Befehle umzusetzen.

Lage:

„Feind 50 m geradeaus, kleines Gehöft, Maschinengewehrschütze im ersten Stock."

Auftrag:

„Wir müssen Anhöhe hinter dem Gehöft erreichen, da sich dort eigenen Truppenteile befinden."

Durchführung:

„Dazu: Gruppe 1 umfasst Gehöft links durch die Senke, dringt in Gebäude ein und schaltet Maschinengewehr aus. Gruppe 2 bindet das Maschinengewehr währenddessen durch eigenes Feuer."

Befehle können auf das Nötigste reduziert sein, wie dieser hier in einer akuten Gefechtssituation. Denn natürlich ist nicht die Zeit, die Situation ausführlich zu analysieren, um sie dann konzentriert aufs Papier zu bringen. Vielmehr kommt es darauf an, die Situation schnell zu erfassen, zu bewerten und dann rasch und kontrolliert, die richtigen Maßnahmen abzuleiten. Dabei hilft die Denkweise der Lagebeurteilung und dann der Rhythmus des Befehlsschemas, der die eigene Absicht klar und strukturiert vermittelt. Dieses gedankliche Ordnen chaotischer und unübersichtlicher Situationen wird Offizieren und Soldaten eingebläut – unter Stress und widrigsten Bedingungen.

Fest verankert

Je mehr es beim Erlernen dieser Vorgehensweise drunter und drüber geht, desto leichter lässt sie sich in ruhigeren Situationen anwenden. Drill in der Ausbildung führt dazu, diese Inhalte jederzeit abrufen zu können. Viele Soldaten erlernen sie in einem Alter, in dem sie sich auch als junge Erwachsene noch entwickeln und werden dadurch wesentlich geprägt. Ein Vorteil, von dem sie in ihrem weiteren Leben in vielen Situationen profitieren können – bewusst oder unbewusst – und aus dem auch Nichtsoldaten lernen können.

Struktur trifft Kreativität
Im Zivilleben gibt es viele Bereiche, in denen so genannte militärische Tugenden verpönt sind und schon fast etwas Anrüchiges haben. Marketing, Kommunikation, eigentlich überall, wo Kreativität, ausgefallene Ideen und unorthodoxe Herangehensweisen gefragt sind. Hier fängt man gerne einfach mal an zu machen, Aktion wird oft wichtiger, als die zugrunde liegende Planung. Gerade in Zeiten, in denen Schlagworte wie Digitalisierung und Agilität den Alltag beherrschen, wird leider oft der Weg zum Ziel, was wiederum dazu führen kann, dass Aktivitäten wenig zielgerichtet und miteinander vernetzt ablaufen (Abb. 2.3).

Kreativität baucht Richtung
Kreativität bedeutet schöpferisch oder gestalterisch zu arbeiten und ist natürlich unverzichtbar – gerade in den genannten Berufsfeldern. Richtig zur Wirkung

Abb. 2.3 Kreativität und Chaos gehören nicht zwingend zusammen

kommt sie allerdings erst, wenn sie sich innerhalb gewisser Leitplanken entfalten kann und damit Richtung erhält. Strukturierte Vorgehensweise kann genau diese Leitplanken bieten und widerspricht Kreativität somit nicht, sondern verhilft ihr erst zu einer soliden Basis und wirklicher Schlagkraft.

Chaos als die Regel
Leider sind fehlende Struktur und ein wenig Chaos keine Seltenheit. Das gilt leider nicht nur für die Kreativbranche. Die Bandbreite reicht hier von Aktionismus, der oft die übergeordnete Zielsetzung außer Acht lässt, bis hin zu kleinlicher Detailverliebtheit und zu starker Fokussierung auf singuläre Aufgaben, die das große Ganze ausblenden. Jeder, der schon Projekt- oder Programmmanagementstrukturen kennen lernen durfte, wird vielleicht die Erfahrung gemacht haben, dass auch ausgefeilte Projektmanagementtools oft zum Selbstzweck werden können, sodass die Choreografie der korrekten Projektabwicklung die Lösung der eigentlichen Aufgabe schnell in den Hintergrund drängen kann.

Offiziere im Vorteil
Ehemalige Offiziere schlagen sich im zivilen Berufsleben zu meist recht gut. Das hat das Zentrum für Militärgeschichte und Sozialwissenschaften der Bundeswehr, in einer empirischen Studie zu Karriereverläufen von Zeitsoldaten am Beispiel ehemaliger Offiziere im Jahr 2017 als Fazit gezogen. Als Gründe hierfür werden gemeinhin Entscheidungsfreude und die Bereitschaft, Verantwortung zu übernehmen genannt. Beides ist sicherlich richtig, kommt aber in der Regel als Teil des Gesamtpakets „richtiges Mindset" daher, dessen Grundlage genau die geschilderte Denkstruktur ist. Selbstverständlich lösen sich ehemalige Soldaten im Laufe der Zeit vom allzu militärischen Jargon, der mit Begriffen wie „Kampfkraft", „Feindlage" und „Führungs- und Fernmeldewesen" gespickt ist. Und auch das strenge Schema lockert sich mit der Zeit auf. Basis bleibt dabei aber die verinnerlichte Denkweise, meist angereichert mit zivilen Techniken. Denn selbstverständlich gibt es auch hier nützliche Tools. Prinzipien und Instrumente ergänzen sich, meinen mit unterschiedlichen Bezeichnungen oft dasselbe und entfalten vor allen Dingen in Kombination ihre volle Kraft. Zivil-militärisch-interdisziplinär zu denken erscheint einfacher als es in Wirklichkeit ist. Denn Zivilisten schieben alles Militärische schnell in die tumb-bürokratische Kommissecke, während Soldaten über Kreativitätstechniken, psychologische Erkenntnisse und sonstiges gerne die Nase rümpfen. Legt man hier die Scheuklappen ab und geht unvoreingenommen an Erkenntnisse „beider Welten" heran, erhält man ein starkes Instrument in seiner Problemlösungs-Werkzeugkiste, das sowohl im Arbeitsalltag, als auch im Privatleben weiterhilft.

Muss es immer Planung sein?

Muss man alles planen? Kann man stattdessen nicht einfach loslegen? Plan, Struktur, Schema – was kommt als Nächstes? Knicken, lochen und abheften? Klingt doch alles ziemlich langweilig, angestaubt und deutsch, oder? Diese Einwände haben alle eines gemeinsam: Sie sind Entschuldigung und gleichzeitig Startschuss für Aktionismus. Denn sie unterstellen, dass Dinge „überplant" und damit komplizierter werden, als sie es ursprünglich waren (Abb. 2.4). Tatsächlich gibt es genug Menschen, die munter drauflosarbeiten. Das kann manchmal gut, könnte aber eigentlich immer besser gehen, wenn man sich zumindest kurz die Zeit für ein Mindestmaß an Planung nimmt. Mindestmaß zeigt es schon: Bei Planung gibt es zahlreiche Zwischentöne. Denn es ist sicher nicht hilfreich, vor jedem Schuhkauf die Checkliste zu zücken, vor der Wahl des abendlichen Fernsehprogramms den Familienstrategiekreis einzuberufen oder jede Fragestellung mit einer Arbeitsgruppe zu beantworten. Zu planen, heißt strukturiert vorzugehen und sich vor der eigentlichen Aktion über diese Struktur Gedanken zu machen. Das kann detailliert sein, z. B. wenn es sich an dem gezeigten Befehlsschema orientiert. Es kann sich aber auch blitzschnell, nur in Gedanken und innerhalb weniger Sekunden abspielen. Oft kann man es auch einfach mal sein lassen mit der Planung und anfangen, ohne lang zu überlegen. Nur sollte die Situation passen und man sollte es als bewusste Ausnahme und nicht als generelle Herangehensweise wählen.

Unklare Ziele

Auch Ziele müssen nicht immer bis ins letzte Detail klar sein. Das ist immer öfter schlichtweg nicht möglich. Dann geht es nicht anders, als in die grobe Richtung aufzubrechen und zu handeln, bis das Ziel unterdessen immer klarer

Abb. 2.4 Keine Angst: Das Leben ist kein Hängeregister

wird. Im Zuge der Digitalisierung haben sich vollkommen neue Planungs- und Arbeitsformen entwickelt, die diese Vorgehensweise ins Zentrum stellen. Aber selbst hier startet alles mit einem Ziel und wenn es nur darin besteht, es auf dem Weg dahin zu schärfen. Auch in dieser Form des agilen Arbeitens ließ sich das ein oder andere militärische Grundprinzip entdecken, das würde aber ein weiteres Buch füllen. Art und Umfang der Planung müssen angemessen sein. Das kann bedeuten, einfach nur kurz und systematisch nachzudenken, knapp die Angelegenheit zu skizzieren oder tatsächlich Stift und Papier zur Hand oder die Tastatur unter die Finger zu nehmen und sein Vorgehen strukturiert zu entwerfen (Abb. 2.5).

Aktiv versus Passiv

In welcher Ausprägung auch immer: Planung zahlt sich auf jeden Fall aus. Denn wer plant, fängt schon einmal an. Planen bedeutet, Situationen vorwegzunehmen, sich auf sie vorzubereiten und Abläufe zu durchdenken. Damit ist man aktiv und ergreift die Initiative. Speziell beim Militär ist Initiative sehr wertvoll und bringt einen in eine vorteilhafte Position. Es gibt zahlreiche Redewendungen, die zeigen, dass diese Erkenntnis auch im Zivilleben Einzug gehalten hat: „Angriff ist die beste Verteidigung", der „Jäger, anstatt der Gejagte zu sein", der „Treiber, statt der Getriebene". Und das gilt für alle Lebensbereiche. Kindliche Strategen begreifen recht schnell, dass es cleverer ist, in der Schule den Finger zu heben, als mit leerem, betont unbeteiligtem Blick auf plötzliche Unsichtbarkeit zu setzen, die einen vor dem strengen Lehrerauge bewahrt. In den meisten Sportarten, von Skifahren über Windsurfen, bis hin zum Turniertanz ist Elastizität in den Knien schon die halbe Miete. Denn damit bleibt man reaktionsfähig, kann Stöße aktiv abfangen, statt passiv und unbeholfen von der Bodenwelle ausgehebelt oder von

Abb. 2.5 Ein Plan kann auch mal ganz einfach sein

der Welle vom Surfboard geschnippt zu werden. Aktion bringt einen nahezu immer in eine bessere Situation. Geht dabei etwas daneben, hat man zumindest einen Ansatzpunkt, den man verbessern kann. Denn man weiß ja, was man bewusst getan hat und was nicht geklappt hat. Wäre man lediglich passiver Spielball der Entwicklungen, müsste man erst raten, wo der Fehler zu finden ist.

Mit Situationen anfreunden

Nicht zuletzt schafft Planung Sicherheit. Wer plant, beschäftigt sich mit der Zukunft und macht sich somit mit unbekannten Situationen vertraut. Unbekanntes wird zu Bekanntem und selbst wenn in der Realität alles anders kommt als ursprünglich gedacht, verleiht das zunächst Sicherheit und beruhigt. Das hat nicht nur eine angenehme psychologische Wirkung, sondern kann durchaus zum wesentlichen Erfolgsfaktor werden.

Vor allem aber gilt: Wer agiert, ist vorbereitet, lenkt und beeinflusst. Er oder der sie hat das Ruder in der Hand, ist nicht ausgeliefert, hilflos oder überlässt Dinge dem Zufall. Das ist natürlich keine Garantie, dass alles wie am Schnürchen klappt, aber es ist zumindest ein hilfreicher Start in die richtige Richtung. Also besser ein schlechter Plan (der sich noch immer flexibel korrigieren lässt) als gar keiner.

Die Struktur

3

3.1 Der Auftrag und die Situationsanalyse

Was Sie in diesem Kapitel finden können
- Die Bedeutung des Gesamtzusammenhangs
- Die Notwendigkeit einer ausführlichen und ausgewogenen Ziel-formulierung
- Den Nutzen einer nüchternen Situationsanalyse

Ist der Auftrag einfach zu formulieren, muss man sich keine grundsätzlichen Sorgen machen, denn dann ist die Welt in Ordnung. Der Auftrag ist das große Ganze, die Sache dahinter, das WHY. Er gibt Sinn und verleiht dadurch Antrieb. Zum Beispiel, ernährt man sich gesund, um sein Cholesterin in den Griff zu bekommen, trainiert, damit man abnimmt, nimmt ab, um ohne Schmerzen Treppen steigen zu können. Man spart, um sich in ein paar Jahren eine Weltreise leisten zu können und so weiter und so fort.

Motivation aber auch Check
Der Auftrag motiviert, dient aber auch als Check, ob man noch auf dem richtigen Weg ist – im Großen wie im Kleinen. Und obwohl er so wichtig ist, wird er doch oft sträflich vernachlässigt. Die Folge sind Einzelaktionen, die alle auf ihr spezifisches kleines, meist kurz-, im besten Fall mittelfristig gestecktes Ziel hinsteuern. Damit nehmen sie kein großes, in der Regel wertigeres und langfristiges Ziel ins Visier und erreichen folglich auch keines. Der Punkt Auftrag

ist ein ganz wesentlicher der militärischen Lagebeurteilung, denn er setzt die Absicht der hierarchisch übergeordneten Führung um. Das ist eine Besonderheit der so genannten militärischen Auftragstaktik. Nach ihr sind die Soldaten so ausgebildet, dass sie aus der Absicht der übergeordneten Führung Folgerung für das eigene Handeln ableiten können. Militärische Auftragstaktik ist ein bundeswehrspezifisches Prinzip und in dieser Form längst nicht in allen Armeen üblich. Sie soll genau die klischeeartig stumpfe Befehl-und-Gehorsam-Abhängigkeit verhindern, denn dank ihr wissen Soldaten stets, wie sie mit ihren Aktionen zum größeren Plan beitragen. Damit sind sie auch handlungsfähig, wenn ihre eigene Führung ausfällt oder sich die Rahmenbedingungen verändern sollten. Den Gesamtzusammenhang zu jedem Zeitpunkt im Blick zu haben ist nicht nur hilfreich, sondern verhindert, sich im Detail zu verlieren. Darum sollte dieser Punkt auch immer die angemessene Aufmerksamkeit erhalten, bevor es in die Tiefen der eigentlichen Planung geht.

> **Wichtig** Jede Planung zahlt auf ein übergeordnetes Thema ein, steht in einem größeren Zusammenhang. Dies sollte zu jedem Stadium der Problemlösung präsent sein.

Der nüchterne und schonungslose Blick der Situationsanalyse
Positiv nach vorne sehen. Zielgerichtet starten. Klare Ziele vereinbaren: Bei all dem Hype um Ziele, wird die Gegenwart oft vergessen. Nur wer die augenblickliche Situation kennt, sich nichts vormacht und sie schonungslos beschreibt, kann sicher gehen, auch die richtigen Ziele zu wählen (Abb. 3.1). Darum gibt unser Schema nicht dem allgemeinen Trend nach, mit der Zielformulierung zu starten. Vermutlich kommt dieser aus der trügerischen Sicherheit, ohnehin zu wissen, was die Situation erfordert. Selbst wenn dies der Fall wäre, schadet es nichts, dieses Wissen noch mal auf den Prüfstand zu stellen. Der gründliche Blick auf die Ausgangssituation führt den Auslöser der eigentlichen Absicht nochmals vor Augen. Was beim Militär die sogenannte Feindlage, also auch die Situation des Gegners, beinhaltet, darf bei uns ruhig ein bisschen ziviler daherkommen: In welcher Situation befinde ich mich? Welches Umfeld umgibt mich? Bin ich zufrieden? Stört mich etwas? Gibt es Menschen, die mir Gutes oder Schlechtes wollen? Ein Blick auf die Ausgangssituation, der auch unbequem sein kann, zumindest aber objektiv, sollte der Start jeder Problemlösung sein. Denn zu starten, ohne den Starpunkt zu kennen, macht es zum Zufall, den richtigen Weg einzuschlagen. Dabei gilt eine der ältesten militärischen Regeln, deren Wert sich zu jeder Zeit und in sämtlichen Lebenssituationen zeigt. Derart deutlich, dass sich auch in ziviler Managementliteratur ein Akronym dafür findet: K-I-S-S.

Abb. 3.1 Wer wissen will, wohin er muss, sollte wissen, wo er ist

3.1.1 Das K-I-S-S Prinzip

Die meisten Menschen haben schon einmal etwas vom K-I-S-S Prinzip gehört und beherzigen es trotzdem nicht. Vielleicht, wegen des Irrglaubens, dass Gutes immer komplex sein muss. Dabei ist es meist umgekehrt: Wirklich geniale Lösungen und Ansätze sehen simpel aus. K-I-S-S ist ein besonders eingängiges und passendes englisches Akronym hierfür und wird unterschiedlich übersetzt: unter anderem mit keep it short and simple (halte es kurz und einfach); keep it simple, stupid (halte es einfach, du Idiot oder oft falsch übersetzt: halte es einfach, supereinfach). Wie es nun im Detail lautet ist allerdings egal, denn seine Botschaft ist klar. Sein Ursprung liegt nicht beim Militär, sondern im Design. Er besagt, je einfacher etwas zu verstehen und zu nutzen ist, desto wahrscheinlicher ist es, dass es der Kunde auch wirklich anwendet. Ein Prinzip, das Steve Jobs meisterlich bei seinem iPhone umgesetzt hat. Für uns ist dabei der Kern wichtig: Einfach ist klar. Klar funktioniert.

Kompliziert gleich fehleranfällig

Mit diesem letzten Satz wären wir dann auch wieder beim Militär. Hier lautet eine Grundregel: Nur einfache und robuste Lösungen funktionieren wirklich

verlässlich. Was filigran, formvollendet und detailliert am grünen Tisch aus-
gearbeitet wurde, knirscht im Schlamm, sprich: es stockt beim ersten unvorher-
gesehenen Problem. Sind Planungen kompliziert, kann es natürlich sein, dass
die zugrunde liegenden Inhalte wirklich komplex sind. Ziel sollte aber immer
sein, sie maximal zu vereinfachen. Das kann unter Umständen auch bedeuten,
der tatsächlichen Komplexität nicht immer vollständig gerecht zu werden. In
der praktischen Umsetzung ist das aber oft das kleinere und akzeptable Übel.
Denn allgemein gilt: Unnötige Kurven und Schnörkel verstellen den Blick aufs
Wesentliche, bremsen und erhöhen die Fehleranfälligkeit (Abb. 3.2). Das K-I-S-S
Prinzip wirklich ernst zu nehmen bedeutet, es bei allen seinen Überlegungen zu
berücksichtigen. Wer es als Lebensprinzip wählt, fährt bestimmt nicht verkehrt.

Für militärische Planung gilt: möglichst geradlinig bleiben, überflüssiges
Schnick-Schnack vermeiden, denn die machen das Leben nur schwer und sind
Sollbruchstellen im Ablauf, die man leicht vermeiden kann. Wer das verinnerlicht, erzieht sich dazu, klar, geradeaus und zielgerichtet zu denken. Das erfordert
eine gewisse Routine und kann bedeuten, egal an welcher Stelle des Planungs-
stadiums, inne zu halten, sich die eigentliche Absicht – den Auftrag – nochmals
vor Augen zu führen und Überflüssiges abzuschütteln. Planung sollte entschlackt
und schlank daherkommen. Beherzigt man das konsequent, klaren sich auch die
eigenen Gedanken.

Abb. 3.2 Gilt leider oft: kompliziert gleich fehleranfällig

Einfach, nicht oberflächlich

Auch hier gibt es keine schwarz-weiß-Lösung. „Einfach" heißt nicht „tumb", „schlampig", „oberflächlich" oder „schlecht durchdacht". Denn tatsächlich ist es alles andere als einfach, Inhalte aufs Wesentliche zu reduzieren und schlank zu halten. Den meisten Menschen fällt es viel schwerer, am Kern einer Sache zu bleiben, Wichtiges von Unwichtigem zu trennen. Es ist bequemer, undiszipliniert abzuschweifen und dabei das eigentliche Ziel aus den Augen zu verlieren. Erzieht man sich entsprechend, fällt es leichter, den Kern einer Sache schnell zu erkennen und sich darauf zu konzentrieren. Das ist nicht nur effektiv und zielgerichtet, sondern es erleichtert das Leben ungemein. Denn zum einen minimiert man die Fehleranfälligkeit, zum anderen setzt man sich nicht mit Überflüssigem auseinander und belastet sich damit nicht unnötig.

3.1.2 Die SWOT-Analyse

Die eigene Lage ständig systematisch zu beurteilen ist militärisch unverzichtbar. Wie stark ist meine Kampfkraft noch? Wie viel Munition habe ich? Brauche ich Treibstoff? Undenkbar, hier den Überblick zu verlieren. Ohne ein regelmäßiges und ehrliches Bilanzieren der eigenen Situation geht es nicht. Auch hier gibt es unterschiedliche Ausprägungen. Es muss nicht immer schriftlich und ausführlich, sondern kann auch nur in einem inneren Monolog verlaufen. Hilfreich ist allerdings auch hier eine feste Gliederung. Sie zwingt einen zu Objektivität und Nüchternheit, denn beides fällt natürlich schwer, wenn man die eigene Situation beschreibt. Dabei gilt doch: Je schonungsloser und kritischer der Blick, desto besser ist man in der weiteren Planung auf alle Eventualitäten eingestellt. Eine gute Möglichkeit, abseits Kampfkraft, Munition und Treibstoff, also im zivilen Business-Alltag etwas intensiver auf die eigene Situation zu sehen, ist die sogenannte SWOT-Analyse. Damit wären wir beim nächsten englischen Akronym, hinter dem sich sich die Betrachtung von Strengths (Stärken), Weaknesses (Schwächen), Opportunities (Möglichkeiten) und Threads (Bedrohungen) verbirgt. Sie dient Unternehmen, vor allen Dingen im Marketing, dazu, die eigene Position im Markt zu bestimmen und darauf basierend eine Strategie zu entwickeln. Auch diese scheinbar zivile Systematik hat ihre Grundidee im Militär, die besagt, die eigenen Stärken zu nutzen und sie auf die Schwächen des Gegners zu konzentrieren.

SWOT als Anhalt

Für unsere Zwecke lösen wir uns von der klassischen Definition der Analyse und sehen sie lediglich als Anker, der dazu dient, alle Seiten unserer augenblicklichen

Situation strukturiert abzuklopfen und gründlich zu durchleuchten: Wo liegen meine Stärken? Worin bin ich schwach? Hat die aktuelle Situation etwas Gutes oder Schlechtes? Gibt es Chancen und wo kann etwas schieflaufen? Beantworten wir diese Fragen nüchtern und ungeschönt, ergibt sich logisch und fast zwangsläufig der nächste Punkt unserer Planung: die Zielformulierung.

▷   **Wichtig** Je nüchterner und schonungsloser die Situationsanalyse zu Beginn, desto besser das Ergebnis am Ende.

3.2   Wo will ich hin? Die Zielformulierung

Zusammenfassung
Die gründliche Formulierung eines Ziels ist unverzichtbar. Denn sie gibt nicht nur die Richtung der Umsetzungsschritte vor, sondern auch wie sie getan werden und ob sie in den Gesamtkontext passen. Dabei sollte ein Ziel stets sinnvoll und ansprechend beschrieben sein, auch wenn das zulasten seiner numerischen Messbarkeit geht.

Was Sie in diesem Kapitel finden können
- Klare Ziele sind robust und verständlich
- Ein Ziel muss sich im wahrsten Sinne des Wortes gut anfühlen
- Die Art und Weise in der wir Ziele formulieren, beeinflusst maßgeblich wie wir sie erreichen

Bücher über Zielformulierung füllen ganze Regalreihen, denn die Art und Weise Ziele zu formulieren entscheidet nicht nur über das Ergebnis, sondern auch über den Weg, der dorthin führt. Dabei besteht ein Ziel idealerweise nicht um seiner selbst willen, sondern leitet sich aus dem großen Ganzen ab – dem Auftrag. Es gibt die Richtung meiner Schritte vor. „Der Weg ist das Ziel" ist dabei zwar eine gute Voraussetzung, auch den Weg zu genießen, sich dabei vielleicht sogar in einen meditativen Flow zu bringen, wird aber im Ergebnis zu wenig führen. Gerade deswegen ist es sehr erstaunlich, dass viele Menschen – im Unternehmen wie im Alltag – diesen Ausspruch von Konfuzius unbewusst zum Leitspruch ihres Lebens erkoren zu haben scheinen. Zu oft scheinen Ziele komplett aus den Augen zu geraten, sofern sie überhaupt im Vorfeld formuliert waren. Bleibt auch der meditative Flow aus, verkommt auch der Weg ohne zu erreichendes Ziel oft genug zum Selbstzweck, der letztlich nirgendwo hinführt.

Relevant oder nicht?

Damit das nicht passiert, ist es wichtig, ein Ziel zu beschreiben, das auch wirklich relevant ist (Abb. 3.3). Das hört sich selbstverständlich an, ist es aber nicht. Natürlich gibt es auch hier Faustformeln, Merksätze, etc., die dabei helfen sollen. Leider besteht die Gefahr, sich ihnen zu versteigen und somit den eigentlichen Sinn des zu formulierenden Ziels komplett aus den Augen zu verlieren. Der wohl bekannteste Ansatz, der die Gefahr birgt, zu absolut sinnfreien Zielen zu führen, kommt aus dem Projektmanagement und ist – wie soll es auch anders sein – wiederum ein englisches Akronym: SMART.

3.2.1   SMART, aber nicht um jeden Preis

SMART steht für **S**pezifisch-**M**essbar-**A**kzeptiert-**R**ealistisch-**T**erminierbar oder, um in der korrekten Sprache zu bleiben, aus **S**pecific-**M**easurable-**A**ccepted-**R**elevant-**A**ssignable (Abb. 3.4). Das soll Ziele auf den Punkt bringen, möglichst

Abb. 3.3 Bei Scrabble nicht der Punktebringer, aber dennoch wichtig

Abb. 3.4 Be Smart

genau beschreiben und idealerweise numerisch nachvollziehbar und messbar machen. In der Welt der Zahlen fühlen sich die Schöpfer dieser Regel vermutlich auch am wohlsten. Nur leider lässt sich nicht jede Zielerreichung so messen und vermutlich wirken solche Zahlenziele auch nur auf Statistiker oder Betriebswirte anziehend und erstrebenswert. Dabei ist genau das unverzichtbar: Ein Ziel muss faszinieren, motivieren und dadurch im wahrsten Sinne des Wortes magnetisch wirken.

Fühlt sich gut an

Das klappt natürlich nur, wenn das Ziel möglichst genau und attraktiv beschrieben ist. Schließlich kann der Weg dorthin durchaus schwierig sein. Was soll anders sein, wenn das Ziel erreicht ist? Auch hier für die Formulierung wieder unverzichtbar: Aktiv vor Passiv – Aktion vor Reaktion. Es ist immer besser, ein Ziel zu erreichen, als etwas zu vermeiden. Wer wird wohl eher abnehmen: Derjenige, der pro Woche 2 Kilo verlieren will, oder derjenige, der nur einen dicken Bierbauch vermeiden will?

Bitte ganze Sätze

Es ist wichtig, dass ein Ziel nicht nur eine Zahl ist, sondern ein Zustand. Und um den zu beschreiben, sollte man ganze Worte verwenden. Die verbinden sich idealerweise zu ganzen Sätzen, anstatt abgehackt als Stichpunkte in der Luft zu hängen – zumindest bei komplizierteren Sachverhalten oder weitreichenderen Zielen. Das kann einen angenehmen und überaus nützlichen Nebeneffekt haben.

Denn selbst bei einem minimal ausgeprägten Sprachgefühl können einem so Ungereimtheiten in der Zielformulierung auffallen. Hört sich das festgelegte Ziel stimmig und rund an? Passt es zur übergeordneten Absicht? Wenn nicht, könnte das einen guten Grund haben. Denn meist liegt der Verdacht nahe, dass der Bruch nicht nur in der Formulierung des Ziels auftritt, sondern im Ziel an sich. Dann sollte man noch mal gründlich darüber nachdenken, bevor die ersten Schritte in die nun definierte Richtung gesetzt sind.

3.2.2   Erzähl mir eine Geschichte – die Macht des Storytellings

Um ein Ziel so zu beschreiben, dass es möglichst ansprechend und damit motivierend wirkt, ist es gut die Technik des Storytellings zu kennen und in Grundzügen einzusetzen. Basis dieser Technik ist der Umstand, dass Menschen in Geschichten denken. Damit schaffen sie Bilder, die Inhalte miteinander verknüpfen und ihnen einen Rahmen geben. Zudem lassen Bilder Emotionen entstehen. Die erlauben es, Anknüpfungspunkte an bereits vorhandene Gedächtnisinhalte zu schaffen – wir können gespeicherte Inhalte somit wieder leichter abrufen. Genau aus diesem Grund prägen Gedächtniskünstler sich zu merkende Gegenstände nicht einzeln ein, sondern legen sie entlang eines imaginären Pfades ab. Sie prägen sich den Weg ein, der dort entlangführt und verketten die abgelegten Inhalte zu einer Geschichte. Damit strukturieren sie ihre Gedanken. Das erleichtert, auf sie zuzugreifen. Sie machen sich damit zudem natürliche, biologische Abläufe zunutze, denn Geschichten führen dazu, dass neuro-plastische Botenstoffe ausgeschüttet werden und die begünstigen, dass im Gehirn neue Vernetzungen entstehen – der Mensch lernt. Sie kreieren und erzählen damit eine Geschichte oder Neu-Deutsch: they tell a story (Abb. 3.5).

Marketinginstrument
Wie der Mensch so ist: Er nutzt biologische Phänomene aus, um damit Geld zu machen. Darum hat das Storytelling seinen großen Hype erfahren und letztlich auch seinen wohlklingenden Namen erhalten. Werbung verknüpft damit Kernbotschaften geschickt miteinander, lädt sie emotional auf und personalisiert sie. Besonders heimtückisch mischt sie auch noch einen Protagonisten, einen „Helden" in die Geschichte. Damit macht sie uns, ihre potenziellen Kunden, zum Akteur, denn Helden sind dazu da, um sich mit ihnen zu identifizieren. Die erzählte Geschichte wird somit unsere.

Abb. 3.5 What's your
story

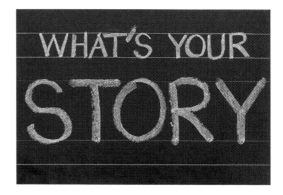

Framing

In Zeiten von Trump und anderen Populisten ist es zwar etwas in Verruf geraten, aber für Storytelling-Zwecke ungemein hilfreich: die Technik des Framing. Wie ihr Name schon sagt, rahmt sie ein Thema und rückt es damit in einen beabsichtigten Kontext. Passiert das entsprechend geschickt, entsteht damit im Gehirn des Zuhörers ein Bild, das die Bedeutung der Geschichte noch nachhaltiger verankert. Gerade die politische Rhetorik ist darin besonders einfallsreich und leider oft erfolgreich. Z. B. entmenschlicht die „Flüchtlingswelle" schutzsuchende Flüchtlinge und macht sie zu einer sich auftürmenden Wasserwand, die sich über irgendetwas unkontrolliert ergießt und es verschlingt. Framing ist, ebenso wie das Storytelling, sehr kraftvoll und entfaltet seine Wirkung auch unterbewusst. Denn die Art und Weise in der wir unsere Ziele formulieren, beeinflusst, wie sie auf uns wirken. Das kann entscheidend dafür sein, wie viel wir Energie wir einsetzen, um sie zu erreichen. Es ist also überaus nützlich, die Wirkung des Storytellings und Framings zu kennen, denn sie erwecken unsere Ziele zum Leben und verleihen ihnen eine Bedeutung. Formulieren wir unsere Ziele ansprechend und in ganzen Sätzen und achten wir darauf, dass wir sie in einen motivierenden Rahmen setzen.

Planning by Bullet Points

Das alles klingt Ihnen zu profan? Im Alltag ist es das leider nicht, denn man spart sich meist den zeitfressenden Schritt des Ausformulierens. Konzepte landen gleich im Office-Programm Power Point, damit sie ansatzlos präsentiert werden können. Also kommen Stichpunkte aufs Papier bzw. die Folie. Tun sich Lücken, Ungereimtheiten und Brüche in der Gesamtgeschichte auf, bemerkt man sie meist nicht, denn sie sie fallen in die Lücken, die Bullet Points nun einmal entstehen lassen. Um das zu vermeiden: Schließen sie die Lücken durch ein Netz ganzer Sätze und formulieren Sie aus, was sie vorhaben, welches Ziel Sie sich setzen. Was Sie nicht in einfachen Sätzen schlüssig beschreiben können, ergibt meist auch in der Durchführung wenig Sinn. Wohl dem, der das erkennt, bevor er sich enthusiastisch-verbissen an die Arbeit macht.

Aktion durch aktive Formulierung
Schon in der militärisch-taktischen Grundausbildung drehte sich alles um „das Heft des Handelns", das es unbedingt in der Hand zu halten galt und die Initiative, die man unter keinen Umständen verlieren durfte. Es ist besser zu machen, als gemacht zu werden. So einfach lässt sich das auf den Punkt bringen. Das beginnt schon vor der eigentlichen Aktion, mit der Zielformulierung. Wer wird wohl angenehmer mit seinen Nachbarn zusammenleben? Derjenige, der versucht, ihnen zu helfen und aktiv auf sie zuzugehen oder derjenige, der sich nur vornimmt, Ärger mit ihnen zu vermeiden? Wer wird wohl gesünder sein? Derjenige, dessen einziges Ziel es ist, Erkältungen zu vermeiden oder derjenige, der aktiv Maßnahmen dafür ergreift, der Sport treibt, Gemüse ist und ausreichend schläft? Worte machen Taten, denn sie beeinflussen, wie wir denken. Auf lange Sicht beeinflusst die Art und Weise wie wir formulieren maßgeblich, wie wir uns verhalten. Das darf man nicht unterschätzen. Wer aktiv formuliert, agiert auch so. Wer aktiv agiert, behält die Initiative, treibt, statt Getriebener zu sein, entwickelt grundsätzlich eine andere Haltung und wird wahrscheinlich erfolgreicher sein, auf jeden Fall aber mehr Spaß haben.

▶   **Wichtig** Die Zielformulierung entscheidet über die Qualität des Ergebnisses und den Weg dorthin.

3.3   Möglichkeiten

Zusammenfassung
Mit der Zahl der zur Verfügung stehenden Handlungsalternativen wächst auch die potenzielle Qualität der letztlich ausgewählten Möglichkeit. Gleichzeitig bedeuten viele Handlungsalternativen auch eine höhere Komplexität der Entscheidung. Hier gilt es, eine zu schnelle Festlegung zu vermeiden, sondern möglichst nüchtern alle sich bietenden Optionen zu untersuchen. Für einen möglichst objektiven, schonungslosen Blick ist es hilfreich, unterschiedliche Perspektiven einzunehmen oder hinzu zu ziehen.

Was Sie in diesem Kapitel finden können
- Wieso die „Qual der Wahl" falsch ist
- Die Gefahr der naheliegenden und offensichtlichen Lösung
- Den Wert des Perspektivenwechsels

Wer die Wahl hat, hat zwar angeblich die Qual, aber immerhin stehen ihm mehrere Möglichkeiten zur Verfügung (Abb. 3.6). Spart man sich die Auswahl, dann im günstigen Fall, weil die beste Alternative auf der Hand liegt, im schlechtesten, weil es keinen Ausweg gibt und Aktion nur in eine einzige Richtung möglich ist. In der Regel gibt es aber immer viele Routen, die ans Ziel führen. Je mehr davon, desto besser. Denn wer die Wahl hat, muss sich vielleicht etwas anstrengen, sie richtig zu treffen. Passiert das aber vernünftig, gilt die einfache Gleichung, in der viele Möglichkeiten auch zum besten Ergebnis führen. Allerdings gilt auch: Je mehr Alternativen in den Blick genommen werden, desto breiter muss dieser auch werden. Dabei neigt der Blick im Gegenteil eher dazu, sich zu verengen.

Abb. 3.6 No_Yes

Scheuklappen sind menschlich
Denn der Mensch will den kürzesten Weg. Erscheint eine Lösung sehr attraktiv, besteht die Gefahr, sich gleich auf sie zu stürzen und andere gar nicht erst in Betracht zu ziehen. Man freundet sich mit der Lösung (zu) schnell an. Das Tückische daran ist, dass diese schnelle Sympathie sich auch auf die Bewertung der Alternativen auswirkt und damit letztlich das Ergebnis verfälscht. Entscheidungen schnell und aus dem Bauch heraus zu treffen sollte die absolute Ausnahme sein. Denn insgesamt geht es gerade darum, die automatisch angelegten Scheuklappen wieder abzulegen und das Blickfeld zu erweitern. Den gleichen Zweck verfolgte bereits die SWOT-Analyse. Wohl dem, der im Team plant. Denn unterschiedliche Personen sehen natürlich auch aus verschiedenen Perspektiven auf Dinge. Ist man nicht Teil eines Teams, bleibt einem nichts anderes übrig, als sich selbst zum Wechsel der Blickrichtung zu zwingen. Das ist nicht so einfach, aber dennoch möglich.

3.3.1 Perspektivenwechsel

Perspektivenwechsel bedeutet, den Blick aus einer anderen Richtung auf eine Sache zu richten. Wie könnte ein Problem auf andere Personen wirken, welche Haltung sich daraus ergeben? Wer könnte davon überhaupt betroffen sein? Welche Lösungen würden sich für sie anbieten. Je mehr unterschiedliche Betrachtungswinkel man einnimmt, desto ganzheitlicher wird der Blick auf ein Thema. Empathie hilft dabei, also die Fähigkeit, sich in andere zu versetzen und abschätzen zu können, was und wie sie fühlen. Das ist anspruchsvoll, aber eine Fähigkeit, die man gar nicht hoch genug einschätzen kann – auch bei der Planung. Menschenkenntnis hilft dabei. Es gibt auch Techniken, die empfehlen, sogar körperlich eine andere Haltung und einen anderen Standort einzunehmen, um sich damit wortwörtlich eine andere Sicht auf die Dinge zu ermöglichen.

Der Blick des anderen
In der Planung geht es aber nicht primär darum, Verständnis für andere aufzubringen. Beim Militär erinnert der Punkt der Checkliste „Vermutete Absicht des Feindes" daran, einen nicht unerheblichen Teil des Befehlsschemas dem Gegenüber, dem Feind, zu widmen. Was hat er vor? Was könnte seine Absicht sein, wie seine nächsten Schritte aussehen? Den eigenen Blickwinkel bewusst verlassen und den Blick des Gegners einnehmen, soll es erleichtern, dessen nächste Handlungen vorwegzunehmen und somit selbst ins aktive Handeln zu kommen. Wie wichtig es ist, Initiative zu gewinnen und zu behalten war bereits wiederholt Thema. Die Welt

aus den Augen des anderen zu betrachten: Diese Forderung klingt selbstverständlich und wird trotzdem selten berücksichtigt. Je stärker Menschen sich auf ihr Problem konzentrieren, desto enger wird ihre Sicht. Das erklärt auch oft die fehlende Toleranz, wenn es darum geht, mit dem Verhalten anderer Menschen umzugehen.

3.3.2 Abwägen

Sind alle möglichen Handlungsalternativen identifiziert und steht ausreichend Zeit zur Verfügung, sollte man sie sauber nacheinander abwägen (Abb. 3.7). Was spricht dafür? Was dagegen. Hegt man für eine Alternative mehr Sympathie als für andere, sollte man das dennoch ausblenden und sie zunächst gleichberechtigt zu den anderen behandeln. Nur so kommt man zu einer vernünftigen Entscheidungsgrundlage. Und wer weiß, im Idealfall bestätigt die möglichst subjektive Vorgehensweise das vorhandene Bauchgefühl. Auch hier könnte man wieder ins Detail gehen und für jede Handlungsmöglichkeit eine eigene SWOT-Analyse starten. Insgesamt soll die Vorgehensweise aber praktikabel bleiben. Also folgen wir dem K.I.S.S.-Prinzip und halten sie bewusst kurz. Wie ausführlich wir vorgehen und welcher Aufwand dabei gerechtfertigt ist, hängt aber letztlich von der Tragweite der Problemstellung ab.

▷   **Wichtig** Die offensichtlichste ist nicht zwingend die beste Möglichkeit.

Abb. 3.7 Abwägen

3.4 Auswahl und Entscheidung

Zusammenfassung

Entscheidungen sollten nicht zögerlich fallen, denn ihre Geschwindigkeit kann unter Umständen ebenso erfolgskritisch sein, wie ihr Inhalt. Nur wenn wir Entscheidungen konsequent treffen, setzen wir auch unsere volle Energie dazu ein, sie umzusetzen. Bei wichtigen Entscheidungen kann eine numerische Objektivierung mithilfe der Entscheidungsmatrix hilfreich sein bzw. intuitiv getroffene Entscheidungen objektiv absichern.

> **Was Sie in diesem Kapitel finden können**
> - Wieso eine entschiedene Entscheidung besser ist als keine
> - Dass Intuition und Bauchgefühl immer ihren Raum brauchen
> - Wieso Objektivität beruhigt

Entscheidungen kann man streng rational treffen, indem man sich schlicht für die Lösung mit den meisten Vorteilen und den wenigsten Nachteilen entscheidet. Es bleibt einem allerdings unbenommen, letztlich doch das Gefühl mitsprechen zu lassen. Denn komplett aus dem Bauch kommt die Entscheidung nicht, der Kopf durfte bis hierhin immerhin alle infrage kommenden Alternativen gegeneinander abwägen.

Setzt sich nun doch Gefühl gegen Hirn durch, passiert das zumindest ganz bewusst und nicht, weil man zu wenig nachgedacht hätte.

Hauptsache man entscheidet überhaupt. Denn viele Menschen neigen dazu, den Schlussstrich der Entscheidung endlos hinauszuzögern. Dahinter kann übertriebener Perfektionismus stehen – die Überzeugung, bis in die Unendlichkeit abwägen zu müssen, um die wirklich beste Alternative zu finden. Oder man hat einfach nur panische Angst vor Fehlern. Bereits unter jungen Offiziersanwärtern kursiert ein recht rustikaler Spruch, der für die Entscheidungsfindung aber ganz elementar ist: „Wenn schon Sch…, dann Sch… mit Schwung." Etwas drastisch fordert er auf, vorangegangene Überlegungen abzuschließen und entschlossen zu handeln, anstatt zögerlich nichts zu tun. Es ist genau diese Eigenschaft, die viele Arbeitgeber an ehemaligen Soldaten schätzen. Nein, nicht etwa, mit Entschlossenheit das Falsche zu tun. Vielmehr geht es darum, eine Entscheidung zu treffen und dann voll und ganz die Verantwortung für sie zu übernehmen. Das beinhaltet, alle Kräfte nun auf die Umsetzung auszurichten und die Konsequenzen, die sich hieraus ergeben, voll zu tragen.

Die Entscheidungsmatrix

Gefühlentscheidungen sind so eine Sache. Selbst wenn man darauf setzt, zu 100 % wohl fühlt man sich in der Regel erst, wenn sie möglichst objektiv unterfüttert sind. Vor- und Nachteile gegeneinander sauber abzuwägen ist ein Schritt, Zahlen mit ins Spiel zu bringen ein weiterer. Das kann vor allen Dingen hilfreich sein, wenn einfach zu viele Faktoren die Entscheidung beeinflussen und die schlichte Auflistung aller Pros und Contras der vorhandenen Komplexität nicht gerecht wird. Eine Möglichkeit, auch Zahlen in die Entscheidungsfindung miteinzubeziehen, ohne dabei allzu mathematisch zu werden, ist die Entscheidungsmatrix. Sie erlaubt es, eine Möglichkeit anhand verschiedener, unterschiedlich gewichteter Kriterien zu bewerten. Dadurch entsteht eine recht objektive Reihenfolge der Möglichkeiten, an die man sich komplett halten kann oder die zumindest in die Entscheidungsfindung miteinfließen kann. In dem folgenden, einfachen Beispiel geht es um die Entscheidung zwischen drei Job-Alternativen (Tab. 3.1). Hier geht man in drei Schritten vor.

Schritt 1:

Zunächst sammelt man Kriterien, die einem für seine Entscheidung wichtig sind und sortiert sie nach ihrer Wichtigkeit. Hierbei erhält das wichtigste Kriterium die höchste Zahl, also das höchste Gewicht. In unserem Beispiel wäre die Job-Sicherheit das wichtigste und das Image des Arbeitgebers das am wenigsten wichtige Kriterium.

Schritt 2:

Im Anschluss schätzen wir die unterschiedlichen Arbeitgeber hinsichtlich der festgelegten Kriterien ein und bewerten sie mit Schulnoten.

Schritt 3:

Diese Note multiplizieren wir mit der Schulnote, addieren diese und teilen sie durch die Summe der Gewichtungen, errechnen somit also ihren Notenschnitt.

Tab. 3.1 Entscheidungsmatrix

Gewicht	Kriterium	Betrieb 1		Betrieb 2		Betrieb 3	
3	Bezahlung	2	6	3	9	4	12
2	Chancen	2	4	4	8	1	2
6	Sicherheit	1	6	4	24	3	18
1	Image	3	3	3	3	4	4
5	Arbeitszeiten	2	10	1	5	5	25
17		Ges	29	Ges	49	Ges	61
Gesamtnote		1,7		2,9		3,6	

Die entstehende Gesamtnote zeigt in unserem Beispiel, dass wir rein objektiv Betrieb 1 wählen sollten und am wenigsten Betrieb 3.

Es steht einem auch nach Befüllen dieser Entscheidungsmatrix frei, letztlich das Gefühl entscheiden zu lassen. Es kann aber durchaus beruhigend wirken, wenn Bauchgefühl und Zahlen in die gleiche Richtung weisen. Tun sie das nicht, kann man sich immer noch für eines von beiden entscheiden, tut das aber dann im vollen Bewusstsein. Vollkommen objektiv fällt eine Entscheidung ohnehin nie. Es schwingen immer Unsicherheiten, Emotionen und Launen mit. Die Entscheidungsmatrix kann hier zumindest eine objektive Hilfe sein.

▷   **Wichtig** Ob auf emotionaler oder objektiver Basis: Geschwindigkeit und Entschlossenheit sind wichtige Merkmale einer Entscheidung.

3.5   Hinterfragen der Auswahl

Zusammenfassung
Der Mensch neigt dazu, schlagartig die Distanz zur getroffenen Auswahl zu verlieren. Das nochmalige Hinterfragen der ausgewählten Entscheidung durchbricht diese Neigung, stellt die Auswahl nochmals gezielt infrage und zwingt zur plausiblen und schlüssigen Verteidigung derselben.

Was Sie in diesem Kapitel finden können
- Den Wert eines möglichst frühen kritischen Blicks
- Den Zusammenhang von Perspektivenwechsel und Objektivität

Der nächste Schritt tut weh. Denn er widerspricht dem natürlichen Drang, sich mit seiner getroffenen Auswahl möglichst schnell anzufreunden. Genau darum vermeidet man ihn auch in der Regel. Dabei sollte man sich noch einmal die Mühe machen und seine getroffene Wahl bewusst zu hinterfragen, sie auf Neudeutsch zu „challengen". Das kann systematisch-aufwendig, idealerweise im Team passieren oder aber auch alleine und nur ganz kurz im Kopf. Entscheidend ist das Prinzip dahinter. Und das ist alles andere als neu.

Seine Ursprünge liegen in einer Organisation, die ähnlich hierarchisch organisiert und schwerfällig ist wie das Militär. Die katholische Kirche stellte mit ihrem „Advocatus Diaboli" alle Argumente und Belege auf den Prüfstand, die für eine anstehende Heiligsprechung zusammengetragen worden waren und die ihr Fürsprecher, der „Advokatur dei", verteidigen musste (Abb. 3.8). Die gleiche Taktik verfolgte – und schon wären wir wieder beim Militär – der preußische Generalstab vor seinen Schlachten. Offiziere nahmen in einer Art Brettspiel Zug für Zug der bevorstehenden Auseinandersetzung vorweg und diskutierten sie durch.

Diese Vorgehensweise erfuhr ihr Revival mit einem Ereignis, das am 11.09.2001 einen weltweiten Einschnitt darstellte (Abb. 3.9). Der Anschlag auf das World Trade Center brachte neue Begriffe ins Spiel wie asymmetrische Kriegs-führung, Waterboarding und auch das so genannte Red Teaming. Die Wirkungs-losigkeit der eigenen militärischen Überlegenheit, auf die man sonst gesetzt hatte, zwang zu neuem Denken. US Militär und Geheimdienst trugen, auf der Grund-lage moderner kognitiver Psychologie, Problemlösungs- und gruppendynamische

Abb. 3.8 Der Weg zur Heiligsprechung war lang

Abb. 3.9 Neue Zeiten – alte Mittel

Arbeitstechniken zusammen. Daraus entstand ein System, mit dem die Planer und Analysten Strategien überprüfen und ihre Entscheidungsträger unterstützen konnten: Red Teaming.

Ziviles Red Teaming
Red Teaming fand mittlerweile seinen Einzug in Unternehmen weltweit. Als „War Games" ist es im Bereich der IT zum festen Bestandteil des Planungsprozesses geworden. Hier werden Teams zusammengestellt, deren Mitglieder verschiedene Hintergründe haben. Diese interdisziplinären Red Teams nehmen dann Annahmen und Pläne bewusst kritisch unter die Lupe und identifizieren so jede noch so kleine Schwachstelle. Im Kern bedeutet Red Teaming also kritisch zu hinterfragen, selbst auf Lücken zu stoßen, bevor sie jemand anders aufdeckt und einen damit in die Defensive bringt. Nur so können, gerade große Unternehmen, ihre eingefahrenen Prozesse hinterfragen und mit kleineren wesentlich wendigeren Konkurrenten mithalten. Red Teaming zeigt uns, wie wichtig es ist, die eigenen Entscheidungen oder hier in unserem Fall die getroffene Auswahl kritisch zu hinterfragen. Dafür nutzen wir erneut unser Storytelling. Wir knüpfen an unsere Geschichte an und erzählen sie weiter. Ist sie noch immer rund? Sind mittlerweile Ungereimtheiten entstanden oder logische Brüche? Lässt sich das, was wir vorhaben immer noch zusammenfassen, sodass wir es anderen verständlich beschreiben könnten?

Perspektivenwechsel
Die kritischsten Fragen fallen uns ein, wenn wir die Perspektive eines anderen einnehmen. Wen betrifft unsere Auswahl? Was könnten der- oder diejenige davon halten. Wie könnten sie meine Auswahl hinterfragen, angreifen und wie würde ich sie verteidigen? Nur wenn die Antwort darauf einfach und unkompliziert möglich ist, hat die Auswahl auch Hand und Fuß – zumindest einstweilen, denn Red Teaming ist ein Prinzip, mit dem man die eigene Planung immer wieder hinterfragen kann. Idealerweise zieht man dafür natürlich andere Personen hinzu, denn denen fällt es natürlich am leichtesten, die Auswahl auf den Prüfstand zu stellen.

▷   **Wichtig** Kritisiere deine Entscheidung bevor es andere tun können.

3.6   Die Umsetzung

Zusammenfassung
Bei der Umsetzung komplexer Vorhaben ist die Devise: vereinfachen und zerlegen. Komplizierte Gesamtvorhaben lassen sich meist in kleinere und einfachere

unterteilen, die es dann diszipliniert und fleißig abzuarbeiten gilt. Abseits des klassischen Projektmanagements mit seinen Strukturen, Meilensteinen und Aufgabenpaketen stehen mit der Mind Map und dem Issue Tree einfache, aber wirkungsvolle Instrumente zur Verfügung, die auf diesem Prinzip basieren. Dabei erhalten ein ausgewogenes Qualitätsverständnis und der effektive Umgang mit Fehlern das Momentum der Umsetzung und sichern so ein reibungsloses und aktives Vorankommen.

Was Sie in diesem Kapitel finden können
- Unterteilen vereinfacht
- Den Fluch des Perfektionismus
- Den Mehrwert von Fehlern

Vorhaben, ob geschäftlich oder privat, wirken oft so kompliziert, dass man sie erst gar nicht anpacken will oder nicht weiß, wo man damit beginnen soll. Ihre Komplexität blockiert, denn eine schnelle Lösung ist nicht erkennbar, was wiederum zu Nervosität und Panik führen kann. Der Wald ist vor lauter Bäumen nicht zu sehen und die Energie schwindet, bevor überhaupt der erste Schritt Richtung Lösung gesetzt ist. Noch dazu ist der Gesamtzusammenhang, geschweige denn das Ziel sofort in all seinen Details zu erkennen. Gerade dieser Umstand sollte immer weniger verunsichern, denn Zusammenhänge werden immer komplexer und flexibler. Das Gefühl der Unüberwindlichkeit sollte man also tunlichst beiseiteschieben, denn letztlich frisst es nur Kraft. Stattdessen heißt es: raus aus der Passivität und aktiv und beharrlich das Dickicht, das sich vermeintlich vor einem auftut, entwirren und somit die Bäume im Wald wieder allmählich sichtbar machen.

Unterteilen führt zu Überblick
Das Zauberwort heißt hierbei: zerlegen. Wenn eine Sache groß ist und unüberwindbar scheint, macht man mehrere kleine daraus und arbeitet eine nach der anderen ab. Solange, bis die große insgesamt erledigt ist. Teilprobleme sind überschaubarer und bieten ein klares Ziel, auf das man sich konzentrieren kann. Das Gesamtproblem verliert damit deutlich an Schrecken und mit weiterem Vorankommen schärft sich meist auch die Zielsetzung.

3.6.1   Mind Map und Issue Tree

Mind-Mapping ist die wohl bekannteste Arbeitstechnik, um Probleme in ihrer Ganzheitlichkeit zu erfassen. Mit ihr lassen sich Zusammenhänge bildlich darstellen und zwar so, wie sie auch das menschliche Gehirn visualisiert. Das macht man sich schon sehr lange zunutze. Denn Mind Maps gab es schon im dritten Jahrhundert. Sicherlich einem anderen Namen gruppierten Philosophen und Intellektuelle grafische Elemente rund um einen zentralen Gedanken und entwickelten so Konzepte, Theorien und Ideen. Heutzutage ist das Mind Mapping an Flip Charts in Besprechungszimmer gewandert und dient dazu, Ideen zu sammeln und zu ordnen. Mit unterschiedlichen Formen und Farben dient die Technik hervorragend zum Brainstorming, also dem offenen Sammeln von Ideen, meist in Gruppen. Es lassen sich damit allerdings auch Zusammenhänge aufdröseln und große Themenstellungen in mehrere untergeordnete kleinere zerlegen (Abb. 3.10).

Auf den Baum mit den Problemen
Überblickt man das Problem etwas besser, lässt sich die nächste Technik anwenden. Mit dem Problem-Baum, dem Issue-Tree, gehen Unternehmensberater oft vor, wenn sie ein Problem erfassen und ordnen, um es in der Folge strukturiert abzuarbeiten (Abb. 3.11). Insbesondere die US-Beratungsgesellschaft McKinsey bezeichnet, die meist im Team erstellten, Issue-Trees als Grundlage aller Beratungsprojekte. Schon Kandidaten, die sich um einen begehrten Consultant-Job

Abb. 3.10 Mind Map

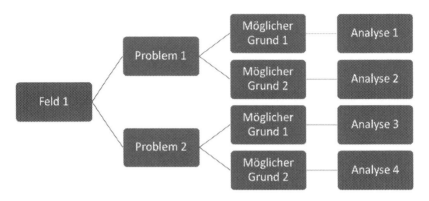

Abb. 3.11 Issue-Tree

bewerben, wird nahegelegt, sich für die Fallstudien, die es im Bewerbungsgespräch zu lösen gilt, mit der Issue-Tree-Technik auseinanderzusetzen.

Das Zauberwort heißt auch hier wieder „zerlegen". Denn der Untersuchungs-gegenstand wird in seine Bestandteile zergliedert. Je komplexer dabei die Sache, desto weiter verästelt sich der Baum. Der Issue-Tree verdeutlicht Abhängigkeiten, Problem- oder Lösungszusammenhänge und auch, wie sich bestimmte Inhalte in den Gesamtzusammenhang einordnen. Dabei kann es zwei Herangehensweisen geben: die problembasierte und die lösungsbasierte. In der problembasierten leitet die Frage „wieso" die Suche nach dem ursächlichen Problem. Im Gegensatz dazu untersucht die lösungsbasierte, wie eine Lösung zu erreichen ist.

Struktur ist Sicherheit

Beide Vorgehensweisen haben den gleichen Kern wie auch militärische Techni-ken: Struktur ordnet und gibt Sicherheit. Mind Map und Issue-Tree portionieren komplexe Fragestellungen in ihre Bestandteile. Dabei muss man nicht zwischen beiden Techniken wählen, sondern kann sie auch miteinander verzahnen. So kann die Mind Map im ersten Schritt helfen, einen Überblick über die Fragestellung, ihre Zusammenhänge und Abhängigkeiten schaffen. Der strukturierte Issue-Tree setzt dann darauf auf, priorisiert und ordnet, die noch chaotischere Mind Map zu einem Schlachtplan, der dann die einzelnen Arbeitspakete zeigt. Alleine durch ihre Vorgehensweise verleihen beide Techniken Sicherheit. Struktur ordnet, Ord-nung beruhigt und macht zuversichtlich, besonders wenn es sich um komplexe Fragestellungen handelt. Weiß man beide Techniken in seinem Werkzeugkasten und hat sie auch schon erfolgreich eingesetzt, lässt es sich wesentlich gelassener künftige Themen angehen.

Schritt auf Schritt

Nicht nur bei der Planung ist System gefragt, sondern auch bei der Umsetzung. Welchen Schritt setzt man zuerst? Die Antwort darauf ist meist gar nicht so einfach. Denn Umsetzungsschritte hängen voneinander ab, sind verwoben oder haben auch mal gar nichts miteinander zu tun. Oft kann auch hier eine Mind Map helfen, um sich all die Zusammenhänge zu verdeutlichen und eine Schrittreihenfolge festzulegen. Aber Vorsicht: Auch hier wieder nicht im Detail verheddern und an Schwung verlieren, sondern die Dinge einfach halten und K.I.S.S. beherzigen. Denn, wie gesagt, oft schärfen sich die Details, wenn man sich schon auf den Weg der Umsetzung gemacht hat. Also kann es gut sein, dass sich die korrekte Reihenfolge der Schritte ergibt, kurz bevor man sie setzt. Es kann auch richtig sein, einfach loszugehen, um so letztlich in Bewegung zu bleiben.

Zusammenfassung

Was Sie in diesem Kapitel finden können

- Vorteil von Planung und Struktur
- Wert von Prägnanz und Geschichten
- Verbesserungen durch andere Perspektiven und bildhafte Vorstellung
- Die Gefahr des Perfektionismus
- Den Wert von Fehlern

Wertvolle Planung

- Selbst schlecht geplant ist besser als gar nicht geplant. Denn im Grunde genommen heißt planen, über etwas nachzudenken und das hat noch nie geschadet.
- Wer plant, beschäftigt sich mit einer Angelegenheit und lernt sie kennen. Das beruhigt und verschafft Sicherheit.
- Planung richtet den Blick immer in die Zukunft und wenn es auch nur ein paar Sekunden sind. D. h. man läuft weniger Gefahr, auf etwas überrascht reagieren zu müssen. Schon unsere Großväter waren sich des Nutzens bewusst: „Wer wagt gewinnt." Sprich: agieren ist besser als reagieren.

Oft absolut unterbewertet: Struktur

- Darum geht es in diesem *essential*. Struktur, Rhythmus, Muster, verschiedene Begriffe, die alle doch dasselbe meinen: eine wiederkehrende Struktur, die sich über Themen legen lässt und diese dadurch beherrschbar macht.

© Springer Fachmedien Wiesbaden GmbH, ein Teil von Springer Nature 2020
S. Schmid, *Was Sie im Alltag von Soldaten lernen können,* essentials,
https://doi.org/10.1007/978-3-658-27762-8_4

- Was groß und unübersichtlich erscheint, wird durch Struktur in kleine über-sichtliche Teile geteilt. Struktur verschafft einen guten Überblick, macht den Wald wieder sichtbar, obwohl er vor lauter Bäumen verborgen schien.
- Strukturiere ich ein großes Problem, reduziere ich seine Komplexität, da viele kleine entstehen, die leichter zu überschauen und zu lösen sind. Diese klei-neren Teil-Probleme schüchtern nicht ein und ergeben meistens sauber abzu-arbeitende Arbeitspakete.
- Wer eine Sache strukturiert, lernt sie kennen. Manche Probleme schrumpfen alleine dadurch, dass sie vertraut erscheinen.
- Jedes Problem lässt sich beherrschen, denn es gibt immer die passende Struk-tur, die es überschaubar macht.
- Hangelt man sich an einer wiederkehrenden Struktur entlang, entlastet man sich, die richtige Vorgehensweise identifizieren zu müssen. D. h. man kann sich auf andere, oft die wesentlichen Inhalte konzentrieren. Strukturen, Rou-tinen, festgelegte Arbeitsabläufe entlasten, denn es gilt, sie „nur noch" abzu-arbeiten. Das ist das große Plus vorgefertigter Checklisten, die unter anderem vor den Starts großer Flugzeuge zum Einsatz kommen. Piloten müssen nicht lange überlegen, was sie alles vor dem Start zu überprüfen haben, sondern hangeln sich einfach durch ihre im Vorfeld detailliert ausgearbeiteten und durchdachten Listen.

Das K.I.S.S. Prinzip

- Wir sollten Sachen möglichst einfach halten. Jeder gedankliche Extra-Schnör-kel, alle notwenigen beschreibenden Erläuterungen erhöhen die Fehleran-fälligkeit. Das heißt nicht, dass alle Lösungen simpel ausfallen müssen. Aber wer „so einfach wie möglich – so kompliziert wie nötig" zu seiner Maxime macht, fährt bestimmt gut damit.

Gutes aus dem Marketing: Die SWOT-Analyse

- Blickt man auf seine eigene Situation, empfiehlt sich auch eine wieder-kehrende Struktur: Stärken – Schwächen – Chancen – Risiken.
- Was ist an einer Situation gut, was schlecht? Welche Chancen und Möglich-keiten bietet sie? Welche Risiken verbergen sich in ihr? Meist haben Angelegenheiten neben einer negativen auch eine positive Seite. Also gehört es zur objektiven Betrachtungsweise, sich auch beide anzusehen.

Ohne Ziel kein Ankommen

- Das Ziel sollte einen Zustand beschreiben, zwingend in ausformulierten Sätzen. Je plastischer wir ihn beschreiben, desto eher können wir ihn uns vorstellen. Auch das erhöht wiederum die Wahrscheinlichkeit ihn zu erreichen. Es kann sein, dass die detaillierte Beschreibung zu einem frühen Zeitpunkt noch nicht möglich ist, sondern sich Einzelheiten erst auf den Weg dahin schärfen. In diesem Fall ist es wichtig, zu formulieren was möglich ist und dann entsprechend flexibel nach zu justieren.

Die Macht von Geschichten – Storytelling

- Menschen denken in Geschichten. Haben wir Dinge vor oder gehen Probleme an, sollten wir unsere geplante Vorgehensweise in zusammenhängenden, möglichst einfachen Sätzen formulieren. Hören sich diese schlüssig und gut an? Können wir sie einfach formulieren? Die Antworten auf diese Fragen können erste Hinweise darauf geben, ob wir insgesamt richtig unterwegs sind.
- Es ist nicht nur wichtig, zu agieren und aktiv zu sein, sondern wirkt sich sogar aus, wie wir Dinge formulieren. Übernehmen wir doch durch eine konsequent aktive Formulierung auch hier schon Verantwortung und gehen in die Offensive.
- Was wir positiv, optimistisch, aktiv und ansprechend formulieren, empfinden wir auch als angenehmer und anziehender. Diese Tatsache erscheint klein, kann sich aber entscheidend auswirken.

Der Blick der anderen – Perspektivenwechsel

- Planung findet nie im luftleeren Raum statt. Sie betrifft uns und andere Menschen. Diese wiederum reagieren und beeinflussen damit unsere Umsetzung. Um hiervon nicht überrascht und vielleicht sogar gelähmt zu sein, sollten wir möglichst früh versuchen, die Perspektive anderer einzunehmen. Wer könnte durch unser Vorhaben wie betroffen sein? Was könnte seine Reaktion darauf sein? Welche Vorbehalte könnten vorhanden sein? Wir sollten uns während unserer Planung bewusst möglichst kritische Fragen aus der Sicht anderer stellen, bevor diese es tun können.

Stell dir vor … – Visualisierung

- Wer Dinge in Gedanken ablaufen lässt, sie schon einmal durchspielt und sie sich möglichst bildhaft vorstellt, der hat sie schon fast erlebt. Davon profitieren auch Leistungssportler. So rast z. B. der Abfahrtsläufer schon vor dem Start gedanklich die Piste herunter und kommt dabei auf eine ähnliche Zeit wie im anschließenden Rennen. In Vortrags-Seminaren empfehlen die Trainer, die ersten Sätze seines Vortrages auswendig zu lernen und sich dabei das Auditorium und seine Reaktionen darauf bildhaft vorzustellen. Psychologen bringen ihre Patienten dazu, sich die Dinge vorzustellen, vor denen sie panische Angst haben und sich so an sie zu gewöhnen. Es gibt unzählige Beispiele für die Vorteile von Visualisierung. Darum sollten wir, wann immer möglich, die Macht unserer Vorstellungskraft bewusst einsetzen. Auch und gerade in der Planung.

Schlechter Perfektionismus

- Die Welt ist nicht perfekt. Darum müssen es auch die meisten Dinge, die wir uns vornehmen, nicht sein. Das ist kein Aufruf zur Nachlässigkeit. Aber wir lassen uns viel zu oft vom zu hohen Anspruch an uns selbst bremsen. Meist ist es besser, kleine Mängel zu akzeptieren und sich weiter vorwärts zu bewegen, als stehen zu bleiben, um einem Perfektionismus nachzujagen, den es nicht geben kann.

Fehler richtig machen

- Meist ist nicht der erfolgreicher, der fehlerfrei durchs Leben geht, sondern derjenige, der besser mit Fehlern umgehen kann. Denn Fehler passieren, darum ist es illusorisch, sie völlig vermeiden zu wollen. Im Gegenteil, die Angst vor Fehlern kann blockieren und lähmen. Bei aller Planungsqualität: Kein Plan funktioniert praktisch so, wie er theoretisch vorgesehen ist. Ein Plan ist vielmehr ein Rahmen, in dem Unvorhergesehenes passieren kann, auf das man reagieren muss. Das können auch Fehler sein, die man analysiert, so aus ihnen lernt und seinen Plan entsprechend anpasst und verbessert. Fehler sind also nichts Schreckliches, sondern gehören einfach zum Leben.
- Fehler als Lernchance greift auch ein Ansatz der US-Eliteeinheit Navy Seals auf: „failing-forward-fast". Hier geht es darum, Fehler möglichst schnell zu begehen, um aus ihnen zu lernen, es neu zu versuchen und somit insgesamt eine rasche Entwicklung zu absolvieren.

Fazit

Insgesamt ist die vorgestellte Technik sicherlich kein Wundermittel, mit dem sich Probleme von alleine lösen. Entscheidend ist vielmehr, dass man sich eine Denkstruktur aneignet, die ein Muster und System über Situationen und

Inhalte legt, die zunächst unübersichtlich erscheinen. Genau das ist ein Kern militärischen Trainings. Viele Bestandteile daraus finden sich auch in zivilen Managementtechniken wieder. Die Problemlösungstechnik des *essentials* sollte eine praktikable Mischung daraus anbieten und somit militärische Erkenntnisse ins Zivilleben übersetzen. Sie könnte es im Berufsleben erleichtern, den Überblick zu bewahren, wenn der trotz ausgefeilter Prozesse und Projektmanagementtools verloren geht. Denn in der Praxis zeigt es sich oft, wie wertvoll es ist, sich regelmäßig zu disziplinieren und die richtigen Fragen zu stellen: Was ist eigentlich unsere Zielsetzung, in welchem größeren Zusammenhang steht sie? Die Technik könnte aber auch darüber hinaus allen helfen, vor Problemen nicht zu verzagen oder in Aktionismus zu verfallen, sondern Herausforderungen sachlich und strukturiert anzugehen. Schon das alleine lässt sie nämlich oft erheblich schrumpfen.

Das Praxisbeispiel

5

Jürgen Siegl will entspannt mit seinen Freunden grillen. Er wohnt mit seiner Familie in einer Reihenhaussiedlung. Sie haben einen kleinen Garten, eine Garage und genug Platz. Die Siegls sind gesellig und haben einen festen Freundeskreis, den sie regelmäßig zu sich nach Hause einladen. Dabei nutzen sie natürlich auch ihren kleinen Garten, in dem sie grillen.

Gemütlicher Grillabend

So haben sie auch heute Abend zwei befreundete Paare eingeladen. Zu diesem Zweck hat Jürgen einen Gasgrill aufgebaut, Getränke kaltgestellt und Fleisch und Würstchen in der Küche des Hauses vorbereitet. Es sind noch zwei Stunden Zeit, die Gäste können kommen. Die Siegls wohnen allerdings nicht in Italien, sondern noch diesseits der Alpen im südlichen Oberbayern. Und da kommt's wie es leider allzu oft kommen muss: Wie aus dem Nichts verdunkeln plötzlich graue Wolken den Horizont und die ersten Regentropfen hängen in der Luft. Was tun? Jürgen setzt sich nicht erst mal hin, skizziert unser Schema und geht es minutiös durch. Aber Jürgen kennt das Schema, hat es verinnerlicht und hangelt sich gedanklich daran entlang. Das alles geht recht schnell, auf jeden Fall schneller als ich dazu gebraucht habe, seine Gedanken hier für uns aufzuschreiben.

5.1 Der Auftrag

Die Siegls wollen etwas essen und zwar nicht nur alleine und um satt zu werden, sondern für vier Gäste, also insgesamt sechs Erwachsene und vier Kinder. Idealerweise haben sie dabei noch einen gemütlichen Abend an der frischen Luft.

© Springer Fachmedien Wiesbaden GmbH, ein Teil von Springer Nature 2020
S. Schmid, *Was Sie im Alltag von Soldaten lernen können*, essentials,
https://doi.org/10.1007/978-3-658-27762-8_5

Dafür haben sie Fleisch und Würstchen eingekauft, ihre Freunde bringen Salat mit. Der Auftrag wäre somit klar und einfach: Grillen und den Rahmen für ein geselliges Beisammensein bieten.

5.2   Die Situationsanalyse

Hierfür bleiben Jürgen noch zwei Stunden. In dieser ein muss er entscheiden, wie er mit der recht wackelig aussehenden Wettersituation umgeht. Es geht darum, sechs Erwachsene und vier Kinder satt zu bekommen, vor Regen zu schützen und dabei maximalen Spaß zu haben.

Stärken
Er hat Essen und Getränke bereits vorbereitet. Eigentlich will er nach dem Essen mit seinen Gästen im Garten sitzen und in den Sternenhimmel schauen. Nachdem der sich aber nun, wie so oft, versteckt, könnten sie sich auch ins trockene Wohnzimmer setzen. Jürgen hat noch zwei Stunden Zeitpuffer, könnte dort also alles vorbereiten. Seine Freunde würden damit vermutlich auch einverstanden sein.

Schwäche
Nur bei rohem Fleisch und kalten Würstchen wären sie wohl weniger begeistert. Der Grill steht nämlich im Freien, sodass er bei Regen unwillkürlich nass werden würde. Jürgen hat auch keine Möglichkeit ihn anders zu stellen. Die Wahrscheinlichkeit, dass es regnen wird ist sehr hoch, aber wer weiß das schon? Es sind schon viele Gewitter über seine Gegend hinweg gezogen. Außerdem wäre doch ein Abend im Wohnzimmer ungleich fader als im Freien, wie er es eigentlich geplant hatte. Und Fleisch und Würstchen in der Küche zu brutzeln wäre doch auch etwas anderes und würde nur halb so gut schmecken.

Möglichkeiten/Chancen
Eigentlich müsste er doch nur für einen alternativen Grillplatz sorgen. Zwei Stunden Zeit sollten dafür locker ausreichen. Oder sollte er das Grillen wirklich generell überdenken?

Risiko
Das Risiko war leider offensichtlich und grollte bereits im Hintergrund: Gewitter und Regen drohten das Grillen buchstäblich ins Wasser fallen zu lassen. Es wäre sicherlich der „Worst Case", vor dem Regen panisch ins Wohnzimmer flüchten zu müssen.

5.3   Die Zielformulierung

Jürgens Ziel liegt auf der Hand: Alle Gäste haben einen schönen Abend, bleiben trocken und bekommen noch dazu etwas zu essen. Das eingelegte Fleisch und die Würstchen kommen hervorragend an, genauso wie die von den Gästen mitgebrachten Salate. Die Induktionsherdplatten der Küche bleiben kalt, alle Anwesenden genießen die frische Luft und lassen sich von dem bisschen Regen den Abend nicht verderben.

5.4   Handlungsalternativen

Jürgen ist unter Zeitdruck, denn seine Gäste rollen sozusagen schon an. Also geht er seine Möglichkeiten schnell im Kopf durch.

Möglichkeit 1
Er könnte alternativ das vorbereitete Essen in der Pfanne brutzeln und seine Gäste im Wohnzimmer platzieren.

* Somit müsste er sich keine Gedanken mehr um das Wetter machen. Sie würden auf jeden Fall im Trockenen sitzen.
* Die Beilagen und vorbereiteten Salate, die seine Gäste mitbringen könnten sie trotzdem essen.
* Allerdings hatten sie einen normalen Herd und nur eine sehr kleine Küche.
* Aus dem Grillabend mit Grill-Feeling wird eine normale Abendessen-Einladung. Kein urig-rustikales, geselliges Beisammensein.
* Mal ganz ehrlich: Würstchen schmecken doch am besten vom Grill, oder?

Möglichkeit 2
Sie könnten das Grillen komplett vergessen und einfach Pizza für alle bestellen. Pizza aus dem Karton auf dem Schoß, das hätte doch auch etwas Rustikales?

* Alle würden satt und niemand könnte ernsthaft etwas gegen Pizza haben.
* Das Grillfesten wäre übrig, die Gäste würden ihre vorbereiteten Salate mitbringen und wer könnte denn bittschön Pizza und Kartoffelsalat essen?
* Pizza aus dem Karton, das hatten sie zu Schul- und Studienzeiten gemacht. Die lagen aber rund 15 Jahre zurück.

Möglichkeit 3
Jürgen könnte wie geplant grillen. Er hatte doch noch ein relativ wasserdichtes Sonnensegel, das er über den Grill spannen könnte. Die Gäste würden ins trockene Wohnzimmer platzieren.

- Der Grill wäre nicht im Regen.
- Keiner müsste auf sein Gegrilltes verzichten und auch die mitgebrachten Salate kämen zum Einsatz.
- Die Gäste blieben trocken.
- Er würde die Küche ins Freie verlagern, persönlich den Abend an der frischen Luft verbringen und so überhaupt nichts von seinen Gästen haben und umgekehrt.
- Richtig urig-hemdsärmelig, aber auch ziemlich einsam wäre der Abend eigentlich nur für ihn.

Möglichkeit 4
Er könnte die Biertische und Bierbänke in seine Garage räumen. Musik kommt sowieso vom Handy und wird dann halt über akkubetriebene Bluetooth-Lautsprecher abgespielt. Den Grill platzierte er nur soweit von der Garage entfernt, dass der Rauch gut abziehen könnte. Darüber würde er das wasserdichte Sonnensegel aufspannen.

- Es wäre fast wie das geplante Grillen. Eigentlich noch uriger, da die Gäste in der Garage säßen.
- Es könnte vielleicht dem ein oder anderen oder besser gesagt der ein oder anderen vielleicht etwas kühl werden. Aber die Gäste wären ohnehin auf grillen eingestellt, sprich würden Jacken dabeihaben.
- Er müsste nun gewaltig in Wallung kommen, um alles soweit umzubauen, aber das war kein wirklicher Nachteil, sondern vielmehr eine Tatsache.

5.5   Die Entscheidung

Jürgen hat die Möglichkeiten tatsächlich recht schnell abgewogen und seine Entscheidung getroffen, denn dies alles fand in seinem Kopf statt. Er will grillen und die Salate sollen nicht umsonst mitgebracht werden. Der Abend soll urig werden und er muss sich dafür jetzt beeilen. Denn seine Wahl fällt blitzschnell auf die letzte Alternative und bei der gibt es noch einiges hin und her und umzuräumen:

Der Abend soll in der Garage und davor unter einem wasserdichten Sonnensegel stattfinden. Er wird wie geplant seinen Gasgrill benutzen.

5.6   Hinterfragen der Entscheidung

Das tatsächliche kritische Hinterfragen seiner Entscheidung findet in Sekundenbruchteilen statt. So groß ist die Tragweite der Entscheidung schließlich nicht. Er will die Gäste in seiner Garage platzieren und davor.

Rustikaler Grillabend
Da sich alle auf einen rustikalen Grillabend freuen, dürfte das kein Problem darstellen. Vielleicht fänden sie es etwas dunkel in der Garage? Das könnte gut sein, er müsste sie also beleuchten. Wäre es den Gästen zu kalt? Nein, es war ein an sich heißer Sommer. Eine kleine Abkühlung wäre ganz angenehm. Ohnehin duften die meisten Jacken dabeihaben. Insgesamt wären bestimmt alle froh, dass sie sich nicht von Wetter schocken ließen. Und keiner hätte seinen Salat umsonst mitgebracht.

Keine Unordnung und Arbeit
Seine Frau wäre auch zufrieden, denn die Küche würde nicht nur kalt, sondern darüber hinaus auch sauber bleiben. Genauso wie das Wohnzimmer und der Rest des Hauses. Schließlich würde sich der Abend in „seinem" Refugium abspielen, der Garage. Aber diese Annahme würde er sowieso gleich mit seiner Frau verifizieren. Eigentlich gefiel ihm seine Idee mittlerweile ausgesprochen gut. Kein Grillabend wie ansonsten, sondern etwas Ausgefalleneres.

5.7   Die Umsetzung

Bei Jürgen muss es schnell gehen, denn schließlich sind seine Gäste im Anmarsch. Aber alles kein Problem, denn es geht ja nicht um Raketenwissenschaften, sondern und eine Grillparty. Trotzdem nimm er sich die Zeit, sich mit seiner Frau zusammenzusetzen und gemeinsam kurz zu brainstormen, was denn nun zu tun ist. Dabei gehen sie, nur gedanklich, die Struktur unseres Problembaums durch (Abb. 5.1).
    Sie müssen sich nun um drei „Felder" Gedanken machen: um alles was mit dem Grillen selbst zu tun hat, um alles was den Aufenthalt seiner Gäste betrifft und um die musikalische Untermalung. So strukturiert Jürgen seine Gedanken,

Abb. 5.1 Erste Stufe des
Issue Trees

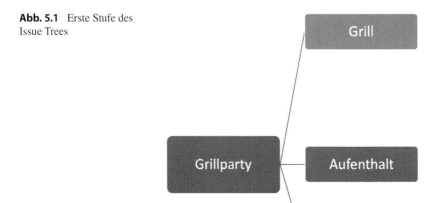

um nun nur noch den entsprechenden Strang seines Issue-Trees sauber gedanklich abzuarbeiten (Abb. 5.2).

So gilt es, das Sonnensegel vor der Garage aufzuspannen und den Grill und die Gasflasche darunter zu positionieren. Als Sitze und Tische müssen alle verfügbaren Gartentische und -stühle dienen. Dabei fällt Jürgen aber auch noch ein, dass sein Nachbar doch auch eine Garnitur Biertisch und dazugehörige Bänke im Keller hat. Sicherlich würde er nichts dagegen haben, sie ihm auszuleihen. Wahrscheinlich hilft er sogar dabei, sie aufzustellen. Als Lichtquelle dienen Petroleumlampen, die er ohnehin in der Garage hat, zusätzlich könnte er ein wenig indirekte Beleuchtung mit einem alten Baustrahler machen, den er auf dem Dachboden aufbewahrt. Falls es doch irgendjemand etwas frisch werden sollte, würde er Decken auf die Bänke legen. Musik ist dank der Mp3-Sammlung auf seinem Smartphone und dem Bluetooth-Lautsprecher das geringste Problem (Abb. 5.3).

Natürlich kann es trotzdem sein, dass Jürgen ein wichtiges Detail nicht bedacht hat. Aber was soll's? Er plant keine Mondlandung, sondern einen geselligen Abend mit Freunden. Da lässt sich natürlich auch noch kurzfristig improvisieren und auch kleine unrund laufende Details sind kein Drama. Dank seiner strukturierten Herangehensweise bleibt Jürgen aber zu jedem Zeitpunkt cool, weiß was er tut und verfällt nicht in planlose Hektik. Er ist entspannt und

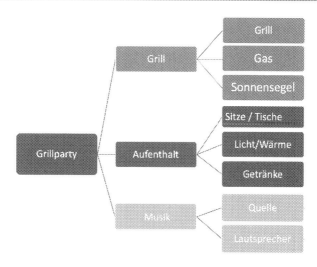

Abb. 5.2 Die zweite Stufe des Issue-Trees

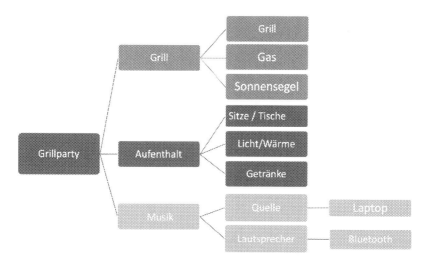

Abb. 5.3 Die dritte Stufe des Issue-Trees

davon hat jeder etwas. Denn keiner braucht einen verspannten Gastgeber, der einem das Gefühl vermittelt, dass ihn der Abend stressen und belasten würde.

Entscheidungen sind subjektiv

Jürgen hat vielleicht anders entschieden, als man es selbst getan hätte. Vielleicht hat er auch nicht den objektiv optimalen Weg gewählt. Er hätte sicherlich seine Gäste auch in die Pizzeria um die Ecke einladen oder das ganze Beisammensein komplett abblasen können. Entscheidungen sind letztlich durch und durch subjektiv. Darum ist die Qualität der Lösung in diesem Beispiel auch sekundär. Vielmehr geht darum zu zeigen, dass ein wenig Struktur und Plan den soliden Rahmen für Lösungen liefern können. Diesen sinnvoll auszugestalten liegt dann beim Entscheider selbst. Das kostet nicht unbedingt mehr Zeit, denn es vermeidet Chaos, das vielleicht ansonsten entstehen würde.

Was Sie aus diesem *essential* mitnehmen können

- Einen Einblick in die Grundstruktur militärischen Denkens
- Die vorurteilsfreie Kombination militärischer Inhalte mit zivilen Techniken – Gutes aus beiden Welten
- Einen einfachen, praxisorientierten Weg fern theoretischer Projektmanagementansätze, der sich aber problemlos mit diesen kombinieren lässt
- Die Erkenntnis, dass bei aller Flexibilität und Agilität ein Mindestmaß an Struktur in Denken und/oder Handeln immer weiterhilft

© Springer Fachmedien Wiesbaden GmbH, ein Teil von Springer Nature 2020
S. Schmid, *Was Sie im Alltag von Soldaten lernen können,* essentials,
https://doi.org/10.1007/978-3-658-27762-8

Printed in the United States
By Bookmasters